DANNY GOT RUN OVER BY A LAWNMOWER

SNARKY STORIES FROM THE DRUNK'S EX-WIFE

Dawn Marie Drake

Contents

INTRODUCTION

Quick Background

I was looking for what every other 40-year-old divorced mom who hadn't had sex in five years was looking for - a fuckin' man. Hopefully one that was single, straight and had a job. Good looks and a sense of humor were just icing on the cake.

I thought I found one.

Danny appeared to be the man of my dreams. He was hot, could make me laugh until tears were streaming down my face, had a great job and could fuck me like a super hero.

By the time I had fallen madly in love with him and was pregnant with our daughter, I figured out he was actually a raging alcoholic with the mentality of a seventeen-year-old who got addicted to everything he touched (except work). He had a little black cloud that constantly hung over his head and had been raining down on him most of his life.

But I loved him! I thought I could fix all his problems and we could live happily ever after. Never mind that he had been in and out of jail for most of his 20's and 30's, or that he didn't have a driver's license because he had been caught driving without one so many times he was branded a habitual offender. I believed that the love of a good woman (me) could fix him.

The day I married him I had an 802 credit score, a chunk of money in savings and a beautiful house. I don't anymore.

Following is some of the absurd things that happened during my time with Danny. Life with Danny would make most women want to slit their throats, but I'm a "roll with it" kind of girl. I try to make the best of situations and find the humor in them.

I was a fuckin' idiot.

"WHAT THE HELL IS *THAT*?"

One night, we were in my kitchen fixing dinner and joking around. I said something funny and Danny threw his head back in a belly laugh. I, being about 7 inches shorter than him, had a fabulous view of the roof of his mouth.

There, in the middle of all those perfectly aligned, sparkling teeth, a characteristic that I was looking for in a man, was what looked like a tiny sequence of numbers on the roof of his mouth.

"What the hell is *that*?" I thought. "Some kind of fucked-up prison tattoo?" I just didn't know. So I asked. I shouldn't have.

He got a funny, embarrassed look on his face. He took a deep breath, and told me he had a partial denture.

"Oh. Okay," I thought. "A couple of fake teeth I can deal with, the rest of them are great."

But, as time went by, the truth came out-apparently like the rest of his teeth!

Turns out, homeboy didn't have a fuckin' tooth in his head! It wasn't a partial denture. Oh no; it was a full set of removable, old people dentures!

That was a shocker I wasn't expecting.

It was a while before he took them out in front of me, but when it finally happened, holy shit! My hot man looked older than my dad! His square, movie star jaw was all caved in and he talked funny.

I was so horrified when I saw his naked mouth, my coochie shriveled up and died a little.

THE PARTY TREE

Danny loved to tell me stories about the good ole days; especially the one about the Tree.

The first month I dated him, I had to hear over and over again about this tree he and his friends used to visit.

He said it was hollow, and big enough for all of them to get inside and smoke their weed. He really, really wanted to show it to me and my four-year-old daughter, Annie.

I avoided this day trip like the plague. I don't like outside. I really don't like outside in the woods in the middle of the fuckin' winter.

One day, he could wait no longer. He was busting at the seams, dying to show us this goddam tree. I should've faked sick.

We got in the car, and I had to drive for almost an hour. Out of nowhere, he told me to pull over and park. I didn't see a parking lot, but managed to find a safe place on the shoulder. All I could see before me was tangled underbrush, thick woods and snow on the ground. Sweet Jesus.

"How in the world are we gonna find a single tree in *that*? You haven't even been here in forever," I said.

"I'll find it," he said, opening the car door. "Let's go; it'll be fun!" He was so damn happy.

3

The last thing I wanted to do was go on a hike. I was trying to change his mind, but my daughter was getting out of the car, so I had no choice; I got my big ass out too.

Five minutes into our journey I was miserable. Nature was kickin' my ass and I just wanted to go home.

It took him a while to find the tree, but he did; which shocked the shit out of me. Listening to all his stories, I had pictured one of those giant Redwoods that people drive through. This was just a plain old tree with a fuckin' hole in it. A hole that didn't look big enough for my ass to fit through if he wanted us to go inside.

But of course he wanted to go inside. He didn't drag us all this way just to look at it; we needed the full experience, he said.

Not wanting to admit I was most likely too fat to fit, I told him there might be snakes or other creatures lurking inside.

"No problem", he said, he would go in first and check it out. So in the hole, he wiggled.

After about ten seconds, his happy ass head popped back out and said all was clear. So I lifted Annie up, and passed her through the hole.

The hole was level with my chest, so again, trying to get out of going inside, I told him my arms weren't strong enough to lift my weight; I would just wait out here. I just knew I would get stuck in that hole and didn't need that humiliation in front of my new boyfriend.

But, where there's a will... He climbed back out to help me.

He weaved his fingers together to make a basket for me to step in, then boosted me up. I peaked in the hole and could barely see my baby through all the gloom.

I stuck my arms in and started wiggling through the hole. Then, what do you know, my fat ass got stuck. I was half in and half out of the tree, just like Winnie the fuckin' Pooh.

Danny was pushing and pushing, but I wasn't budging. Then I didn't feel his hands anymore.

"Where'd ya go?" I yelled.

"Hold on. I'm taking a picture," he said, laughing.

"Get your ass over here and get me out!" I screamed.

"Hold up," he said. "You just need to turn sideways then I think you'll fit."

"Son of bitch," I said to myself, embarrassed half to death.

I turned sideways the best I could, and he shoved me through the hole. I tumbled in, and he quickly followed.

The three of us sat there like Indians in a teepee. The floor of the tree was so cold; it was like sitting on a block of ice. Not having any weed like back in the day, Danny reached into his pocket and produced a can of beer.

"Dear God," I thought, "he was reliving his childhood and we could be stuck here all fuckin' day."

"See how big it is in here," he said in awe, drinking his precious beer.

Well, we didn't bring a flashlight, so, no, goddammit, I couldn't see how big it was in here; I could see my breath though.

Poor little Annie started to shiver, so I put her on my lap to try to keep her warm. We suffered through a few stories about shit that happened twenty years ago, then I jumped up and said it was time to go. My ass was frozen solid, and I was worried my car had been towed.

Getting me out was a living hell. The tree was up on a hill with lots of roots growing all around it. Danny had to balance on the roots to pull me out and since he was half lit, he lost his balance. Down we went.

My ass trying to wiggle into Danny's "Party Tree"

MY HANDY-MAN

My house is about 100 years old, so it's not perfect, but I like it that way. Its heated by hot water that runs through pipes in baseboards around the floor. Every winter, the main level is cold and the upper level is like a sauna. I was okay with that; I just wore a sweatshirt.

Well, Danny wasn't okay with it. He said there must be air in the pipes and he could fix it. I believed him; he had proved to be very handy around the house. He could fix everything else, why not the pipes too?

I was in the kitchen fixing dinner, when I heard him yell, "OH SHIT!" I went running into the living room to find water shooting out of the heat pipe like a geyser, spraying all over everything.

He got down on the floor and tried to plug the hole with his hand, but that just made it squirt sideways, soaking him. He started screaming for me to find him a screw.

"What good was a fuckin' screw gonna do?" I thought, watching as the water saturated my snow white couch. I was ready to kill him. I didn't know what else to do though, so I ran to the junk drawer and found him a screw.

He managed to plug the hole with it and stop the leak, but by then my furniture was screwed.

4 WHEELIN'

It was Easter weekend. His diminishing brain cells from alcohol abuse would cause Danny to make yet another bad decision in the name of "fun." A decision I questioned, but dumbass me went along with anyway.

Despite not having a driver's license for umpteen years, he bought an old Ford Bronco.

New home construction was going on down the street from his house. All that had been done so far was removal of the trees, so there was acres and acres of open space. Danny thought it would be a blast to take Annie and I there and go 4-wheelin' in his Bronco. He promised we'd have a great time.

Visions of that "great time" we had in that fuckin' tree flashed through my mind. But, not wanting to disappoint the love of my life, I agreed and belted my little girl, dressed in her new spring outfit, into the backseat. At least it was warm outside.

Now, this older Bronco was the kind that had a removable top. Since it was a beautiful, warm, sunny day, Danny decided to take it off. This left the cargo space and the backseat, where Annie sat, open. I told her to hold on, and I drove us down the street.

The first thing I noticed about our "playground", was that it was really, really muddy. The second thing I noticed, was that way out yonder, a truck was stuck in the mud and two young men were trying to get it out.

I, the voice of reason, told Danny we probably shouldn't go 4-wheelin' or we would end up like them. He, not having any sense and wanting to show off his driving skills said it would be fine; he could handle the mud.

With a great deal of apprehension, I hopped out and traded places with him. I buckled my seatbelt, and he turned the radio up loud enough to hear it over the thundering engine. Into the field we went to have our "fun."

Not two minutes after he drove into that field, the goddam truck got stuck!

"I told you this shit would happen," I said. He told me not to worry, that he could get us out.

After several tries of rocking the truck back and forth, and going nowhere, my brilliant, future husband decided to just lay on the gas. Screams of panic ensued from the backseat.

I looked back in horror to see my beautiful daughter being sprayed with the chunks of cold, wet mud that were flying through the air, being thrown from the spinning tires. The poor little thing had her eyes squeezed shut, and her body tensed up; she didn't understand what the hell was happening to her. There were pieces of mud clinging to her ponytail, spotting her face, and polka dottin' her brand new clothes.

The revving of the roaring engine, on top of the blasting stereo, almost drowned out my hysterical screams of "STOP."

"What's wrong?" he asked, not being able to hear Annie's cries over all the noise.

"Look what you did to my baby!" I screamed as loudly as I could. "Turn the fuckin' truck off!"

He turned in his seat, and took in the aftermath of his asinine decision to take the top off.

"Oh no," he said. He looked truly shocked that this had happened. "I'm so sorry."

So there we were; child crying, covered in mud and traumatized. The piece of shit truck, sunk in even deeper from all the tire spinning. And we were far enough from the street that I just knew getting there was gonna be a royal pain in my ass. I was pissed!

After finally convincing the man, who thought he was invincible and could do anything, that he really couldn't get us loose, we jumped out to walk back to the house. When my feet hit the ground, I immediately sank at least four inches into the mud.

I heard a squishy, sucking noise when I pulled my foot out, and snap! My fuckin' flip flop broke.

I flung my broken shoe across the field as hard as I could, and pulled my other foot out, leaving that shoe buried in the mud. I opened the back door to retrieve Annie, resigned to the fact that all the mud that covered her was gonna smear on me, but I had no choice.

Her added weight sank me even deeper and was throwing me off balance. Fuckin' Danny tried to take her, but she didn't want anything to do with him.

By the time I carried my daughter back to the street, I had no shoes, my clothes were damp and filthy, my feet were caked with mud and I was thoroughly exhausted from carrying my child through the equivalent of fuckin' quicksand. I got in my car and went home while he looked after me with a confused, dumbass look on his face.

"WHERE'D MY TEETH GO!?!"

One morning, well, early afternoon, after an especially hard night of drinking, Danny was yelling for me to come upstairs. He sounded like it was an emergency, so I raced up to the bedroom.

I found him in his underpants, frantically ripping the bedding off the bed, shaking out the blankets. I could see the panic on his puffy, hungover face and his eyes were wide with fear. I knew it must be something bad, so I started shaking blankets, too.

"What are we looking for?" I asked.

"I lost my teeth!" he exclaimed. "They were in my mouth when I went to sleep; now they're gone!"

Sweet baby Jesus. Only Danny, I thought, shaking my head. What an idiot.

So, he on one side of the bed, and me on the other, started going through the bedding, blanket by blanket. Then we looked under the bed. Then we looked around the bed. I knew the little bastards had to be there somewhere.

Then it happened. He turned around. Hangin' on his naked back, was his goddam teeth, stuck on with pink, gooey Fixadent. Too hungover, or maybe still a little drunk, the fuckin' man couldn't feel them biting into his shoulder blade.

That was the first time drunk Danny lost his teeth.

THE SWIMMING POOL

Our town didn't have a public swimming pool so that first summer
we were together we bought an above ground pool that was about
three feet deep and fifteen feet around; a good size for four-year-
old Annie.

Unfortunately, our back yard isn't exactly level; it goes
slightly downhill from the house to the back fence. We walked
around the yard, trying to find the flattest part to set up our new
pool. Danny decided on a spot close to the house. I didn't agree,
but let him have at it.

The next day was steamy, so I put Annie in her swimsuit
and popped her in the pool. I sat in a chair next to her and
watched.

A while later, Danny woke up and came outside with his
breakfast beer, decked out in his swim trunks. He got in to play
with her while I went inside to cool off and do the dishes.

I watched them having a good time through the window.

Then I watched as Danny leaned over the side to grab his
precious beer off my chair and the whole fuckin' pool collapsed.

Hundreds of gallons of water gushed out, and poor little
Annie was washed away.

THE ROOSTER, THE CHICKENS AND THE DOG

One day, we decided to go to the flea market.

I'm not sure how it happened, but by the time we left, I was the proud owner of two live chickens and a fuckin' rooster.

On the drive home, I pulled up next to a man who happened to have his Chihuahua sitting in his lap, looking out the window. Danny thought it would be funny to sit his rooster on his lap and let it look out the window at the dog.

I was flying down the road, trying to stay even with the other car. The animals were staring at each other and Danny was laughing his ass off. I really didn't think it was funny; until the rooster decided to shit on Danny's pants. That, I thought was funny.

Later that day, my ex-husband brought Annie home. Danny was so excited for her to see her new pets, he let them run loose in my house so she would see them when she first walked in.

She was thrilled. She got down on the floor to pet them, while my ex-husband looked at me like I had lost my mind.

Then one of the chickens took flight. It soared around the room looking for an open window, then flew right into the spinning ceiling fan. When she hit, it wasn't pretty. The poor thing smashed against a blade that held her for half a revolution, then flung her against the wall. She hit the floor like a ton of bricks, but lived anyway.

Danny built a chicken coop in one of my sheds and they stayed outside from then on. It didn't take long for Annie and I to grow bored with them. The chickens weren't laying eggs and the rooster didn't even cock-a-doodle-doo. I wanted to get rid of them, but Danny loved them.

One day he was feeding them, and the black chicken flew into the neighbor's yard.

"Let her go; she wants to be free," I yelled, then started singing the song "Born Free" at the top of my lungs.

He gave me a dirty look, hopped the fence and somehow caught her. He didn't want her to get away again, so he clipped her wings. And she bit him. And I laughed. I just wanted them to go away; they were a pain in my ass.

One day, while Danny was rototilling the garden, our lab, Twinkie, and I went out to feed the chickens. The black chicken, who couldn't fly anymore, wandered out of the coop. Well, Twinkie saw dinner and started barking and running towards her. The chicken saw her coming and tried to fly away. When her wings didn't work, she started running. Danny's back was towards us, and the machine was so loud, he was oblivious to the situation.

The chicken ran past Danny. Then the dog ran past Danny. He dropped the rototiller and started chasing both of them. I had no idea a fuckin' chicken could run so fast.

Danny couldn't catch up with the dog and the dog couldn't catch up with the chicken. They were all running around the yard like maniacs; the dog barking and Danny screaming. My belly hurt, I was laughing so hard.

Twinkie finally trapped the chicken up against the fence, and before the dog could take a bite, Danny saved her. Then I got a lecture.

THE PLAYHOUSE

That August, Annie would turn five. I had figured out just how handy Danny was by then. He could fix anything, except the heating pipe, so I figured he could build anything.

I wanted to do something big for her birthday. We were both still working and rolling in money, so I decided she should have a playhouse in the backyard. Not any playhouse, mind you; not one of those one room, plastic ones you buy at the store. No, my little princess had to have every little girl's dream playhouse; like the one I always wanted, but never got.

Danny said he could build it, so I drew him a picture of what I wanted. I told him it needed to be big; about 14 feet by 12 feet. I also wanted him to put in a loft, so she could have a nursery for her dolls. And I wanted it to look like it came out of a storybook.

So, we went to the Home Depot, and construction began. God bless him; beer in hand, he worked on that thing every night and every weekend. I would sit out back and watch him work, amazed at the things he knew how to do.

On the weekends, when he got really drunk, and I was scared he might mess up my playhouse, I would ask him to stop. But he thought he was superman when he was drinking, and told me he was fine. He always thought he was fine when he had beer in him, no matter what.

One day, I was watching him from the kitchen window. The walls were up and it was time to put the roof on the playhouse. I had no idea how he was gonna do it by himself.

He leaned a huge piece of plywood against the outside wall and set the ladder up next to it.

I watched him climb up the ladder, one handed, because he was taking his beer with him. He balanced his cup on the top rung. He managed to lift the plywood up and lay it on the rafters; a feat in itself. He was digging around in his tool belt for some nails, and I don't know if a gust of wind came through or what. One minute he was standing on the ladder, and the next, the plywood had lifted up, and was pushing him and the ladder backwards. The plywood slapped down on him like a fly swatter.

It looked comical, and I couldn't help but laugh, but went to check on him anyway. Drunks must not feel anything, because he was fine. I would have had to go to the hospital. He went on to fall off the roof a few more times.

When he finally finished, it was spectacular. He did a great job, or so I thought. His intoxicated mind didn't realize he was supposed to use pressure treated wood. The beautiful playhouse eventually fell into disrepair. You could feel the floor crunching underneath the carpet when you walked on it. One day, I went up on the porch and fell right through the floor. Now it's just another eyesore in my backyard.

FIRST FIGHT

We were at my house and I was trying to get him to cut back on his drinking. He said he was a grown man and could do what he wanted; that he was *fine.* I was sick of hearing how fuckin' fine he was; he wasn't fine.

So, we got into it, and out of the blue, he said, "Fuck You!"

"Fuck me?" I thought, "Oh, hell no!"

I grabbed my jacket and keys and told him to get in the car.

"Where are we going?" he asked, confusion clouding his eyes. I guess he thought it was okay to say "Fuck You" to me. It was not.

"I'm takin' your ass home."

"Why?"

He really didn't know.

"Because, you drunk idiot, you said 'Fuck You' to me. Now you're going home."

"Fine," he said, and walked out the door.

We got halfway to his house and he started apologizing. I didn't give a shit; I was pissed and needed to set a precedence. If this alcoholic asshole thought he could talk to me that way, he was sadly mistaken.

I pulled in his driveway, next to his roommate's brand new pickup truck.

"Get the fuck out," I said.

"Come on, Dawn. I said I was sorry."

"I don't care. Get out."

He got out and slammed the door. I started backing up. He couldn't believe I was actually leaving, but I kept going. It was a pretty long driveway and I had to go slow since I can't drive backwards worth a damn.

When I got halfway to the street, I saw him pick up a mechanic's jack that weighed about a hundred pounds, and wing it through the air. I don't know if he was aiming or throwing blindly, but it slammed right into the side of his roommate's brand new pickup truck.

"My Head, My Head!"

It was time for Danny's old Bronco to be moved to my house. His old roommate came over and took us back to her house so I could drive it home.

The damn thing was a piece of shit! It needed shocks, so I was bouncing so much, I was getting car sick. Danny was drunk, so he didn't notice.

On the way home, we had to take a two lane highway that was about ten miles long, with nothing but fields and a house here and there. It was very dark and very late. The engine was so loud, it was hard to think, plus I was about ready to throw up. Then, all of a sudden, the truck just died. I couldn't believe it! I managed to roll it to the side of the road before it stopped.

Danny hopped out of the truck. "Not to worry, honey. I can fix it", he slurred.

Shit! Here we go. He tried and tried, but he couldn't get it started. I wanted to leave it there and never see it again, but there wasn't a car on the road, and it was way too late to call a friend to rescue us.

So we called a tow truck. An hour later it got there, and Danny, being the "Man", wanted to help the tow truck driver.

"No sir; our insurance won't permit you on the truck," the young man said.

I went up by the cab to smoke a cigarette, while Danny stayed around the back and told the man how to do his job. I could see them from where I was standing. Danny was watching the driver secure the chains to his Bronco and I could tell by his body language, he was just itching to help.

The driver had to get back in the cab to start the mechanisms that pulled the truck onto the flat bed. Apparently, drunk Danny didn't think the chains were secure enough and jumped up on the flat bed to fix the problem. The poor driver didn't know this. While Danny was standing up there, at least four feet off the ground, the driver pushed the button.

The floor of the flatbed jolted, and Danny flipped off, head first into the street like an Olympic diver. I gave him a score of 9.5.

God must protect children and drunks, because he didn't die. He was pretty fucked up though. All I heard for the next three days was, "My Heeeeaaad, My Heeeeeaaaad!"

THE POSSUM

One night, we were all in the living room watching TV, when Twinkie started barking to go outside. Danny went to let her out and a few minutes later, I heard him yelling at her from the back door.

"Twinkie, No! Twinkie get in here, now!"

"What's wrong?" I called from the couch.

"She's got some animal pinned against the fence trying to kill it. I think it's a raccoon."

"Well, get her," I said, "it could have rabies."

The next thing I know, in walks Danny, strutting around like a peacock. Beer cup in one hand, and in the other, the ugliest thing I had ever seen.

"Look what the Twink killed," he said, holding it by the tail, high in the air like a trophy. He was so happy and proud of his dog.

That thing was big and pale, with a thick, long tail; it made my skin crawl.

"It's a possum," he declared, turning it this way and that, so we all could get a good look at it.

"Why the hell'd you bring in the house?" I asked. "Take it outside."

"Calm down; it's dead. It ain't gonna hurt nobody," he said, talking down to me like I was some idiot.

"I don't give a flying fuck! Get it out," I demanded.

You know that old saying: playing possum? Well, guess what? His possum was playing!

All of the sudden it started to move, and the worst smelling shit I ever smelled in my life started oozing out of its ass like lava and was plopping on my floor. Me and Annie started screaming, the dog started barking and Danny started jumping around, making the possum swing back and forth. All that motion made the shit, that was still coming out of it, fly all over the place.

"It's still alive!" I screamed, choking on the stink. "Get it out!!!"

Danny ran for the door, slipped in the shit, caught himself, then made it outside. I ran to open the storm door so we could breathe again, and saw Danny at the edge of the street. He looked like a fuckin' cowboy swinging the possum by its tail over his head like it was a lasso. He let go and it sailed over the passing cars into the poor old lady's yard across the street.

BIT MY FOOT

I was sound asleep and woke up to a horrible pain ringing in my foot. I woke Danny up to ask him what the hell he had just done to me. He said he didn't do anything; he was sleeping.

He got up to go to the bathroom, and I laid back down and stretched my leg out. My foot hit something hard, so I reached down and grabbed it. In the soft light escaping from the bathroom, I turned this thing over and over in my hands until my sleepy head realized what the hell it was. It was his fuckin' teeth. I took them to the bathroom, and he looked at them in shock.

"I don't even remember taking them out," he said, bewildered.

Well, I know he didn't take them out cause I watched him glue those fuckers in right before he went to bed. That glue was like cement with a shelf life of at least eight hours.

I still can't figure out how the damn things got from his mouth to the bottom of bed to bite me.

THERE GOES THE OTTOMAN

One night we were watching TV. Danny was sitting kind of behind me on my white chair, using my white ottoman as a table for his dinner-a plate of spaghetti.

I was into my show when little Annie exclaimed, "Momma! What's wrong with Danny?"

I turned around to see the drunk shit passed out cold-keeled over with his face planted in the plate of noodles, sauce spatter all over the ottoman, the fuckin' fork still in his grip.

THE NIGHT HE DIDN'T COME HOME

One night, Danny didn't call me at the usual time to pick him up from the bus stop. I figured he was buying beer and missed the bus again.

He called me at 9:30 that night, told me he had to work late and take a later bus, and that I needed to come to Herndon to pick him up. Even if I paid to take the toll road, it was still a fifty-minute drive just to get there.

Hayley and Annie were both sound asleep, and I wasn't about to rip them outta bed to go pick up his drunk ass, so I told him I was sorry, he would have to find his own way home. Oh, he was pissed.

I thought he would phone a friend, call a taxi, or at least hitchhike.

When I woke up the next morning and he wasn't there, I just thought he got a hotel room; that's what I would have done. He had a fuckin' credit card right there in his pocket and God knows he knew how to use it.

Mid-morning, he came through the door, mad as hell.

"Why aren't you at work?" I asked.

"Hff!" he breathed, looking at me with fire shootin' out his eyes.

"You wouldn't pick me up last night!" he glared.

"The kids were in bed; I couldn't wake them and drag them out in the cold. Annie had to go to school today," I said.

"Well, nobody would give me a ride!" he shouted.

"Did you get a hotel room?" I asked.

"We don't have money for a fucking hotel."

"Well, where did you stay then?"

"I slept in a fuckin' bush! Thanks!" he yelled.

"Why in the hell would you do that?" I asked. I mean, what kind of a moron sleeps in a bush?

"Because YOU wouldn't come pick me up," he said, gritting his fake teeth.

"Why didn't you go to work today?" I asked.

"Because I slept in a fuckin' bush!!!"

Lost 'Em Again!

Danny lost his fuckin' teeth again. This time, I really thought they were gone for good.

We looked high and low, and everywhere in between, and couldn't find the damn things anywhere. Real fake teeth ain't cheap and I was pissed.

I gave up the search and told him maybe the fuckin' tooth fairy took 'em. He didn't find my comment amusing, and spent the rest of his Sunday looking for them.

He wasn't having any luck, and the more he drank, the more he whined.

The next morning, I made him go to work with naked gums. He didn't want to, of course, but fuck him! We needed money; that beer wasn't paying for itself.

Later that day, I was in my room sorting laundry. I grabbed the sweatshirt he had been wearing a couple of days before, now an inside out crumpled pile. I picked it up, turned it right side out, and heard something hit the floor.

It was his fuckin' teeth.

I guess when he was pulling his sweatshirt over his head to take it off, he was smiling or something, and was too drunk to notice the fabric pull his teeth right out of his goddam head.

What a fuckin' mess he was. At least we didn't have to buy new ones. At least not then.

THE AUTO TRAIN

We decided to go to Disney World and to save money, we took the Auto Train.

It turned out to be the train trip from hell; Danny found the cash bar as soon as we got on board.

It was alright at first. We had a nice dinner in the dining car and watched the scenery go by. There was a smoking car in the lower level, so I wasn't having nicotine fits. Hayley was being a good little girl; she had turned three a few weeks before the trip. Danny was sticking to beer and wasn't drunk yet.

But after dinner, he started ordering mixed drinks. Danny and liquor don't mix well. Danny plus liquor plus beer is a disaster waiting to happen.

He started getting loud and overly friendly with the other passengers. While he was being a happy drunk, I knew he was still driving them crazy with his big, fat mouth.

It was getting late and time to sleep. We settled in with our blankets and pillows and reclined our seats. The damn things only went back ten or twelve inches, if that. We were basically still sitting up.

We tried to fall asleep, but it was useless. Hayley was crying and disturbing everyone in our car. I took her down to the smoking car to try to walk her to sleep.

When I got back, all hell was breaking loose. Drunk Danny had decided he was gonna fix the sleep situation. Our train car wasn't full, so he did some rearranging of the passengers. Then his mechanical mind figured how to remove the seats and turn them around to face each other so we could lay across them.

Apparently, this was not allowed. Danny and the train conductor were going at it. Danny was complaining, very loudly and slurring his words, that the seats sucked and no one could sleep. Danny said he didn't understand what the hell the problem was.

"Now we can lay down," he said.

It got so bad, the conductor threatened to throw him off the fuckin' train if he didn't put them back.

LARGE CHILD

Danny taught both girls how to ride a bike. He was a good dad back then. Things that would piss me off and embarrass me, just made the kids laugh.

One day, Danny and Hayley rode their bikes down to the elementary school to ride them around the track. They had the school yard to themselves, which was a good thing. Danny had mastered riding with one hand so his Big Gulp cup camouflaging his beer could be glued to his other one. They rode round and round the track that circled the soccer field.

"Hey Hayley," he yelled, "look, no hands!"

Well, the drunk ass lifted his arms in the air, was looking at Hayley instead of where he was going, rode off the track and ran right smack into a goal post. The bike bounced back and his cup flew in the air. He was thrown off and flew into the net like a fuckin' soccer ball as beer and ice cubes rained down on top of him.

They took lots of bike rides together, and the beer was always clouding his judgement.

One day, Danny decided to take our lab, Twinkie, along. He put her on the leash, grabbed his beer cup, and got on his bike. With Hayley following on hers, they took off down the street.

Danny had the leash around the wrist of the hand he was steering with and his cup in the other. Things were going fine, until Twinkie saw the neighbor's dog in its yard and took off.

She pulled Danny and his bike right off the sidewalk, into one of the deep, rocky gullies that lined parts of it. He lost his beer, and another bike was fucked up.

Another time, they were riding in the church parking lot. Hayley's little friend, who she had a crush on, was riding there too. They were having a good ole time. The little boy was showing off for Hayley by popping wheelies. Then drunk ass decided he was gonna impress the boy by popping a wheelie himself. But, Danny was on a ten speed. You can't pop a fuckin' wheelie on a ten speed; especially when you're drunk and have a beer in one hand.

But, he tried anyway, and went down hard. And lost another beer.

Bikes weren't the only things he wrecked. We were at an estate sale one day and they had a go-kart for sale. He thought our big back yard would be a perfect racetrack and talked me into buying it.

We got it home and the kids were ready to ride. I told him to test drive it first, to make sure it was safe before he put my babies it in.

Without inspecting it first, his drunk ass just jumped in and hit the gas. He was speeding along, having the time of his life, until it was time to turn left. With a loud "Woo hoo!", he turned the steering wheel and the fucker came off in his hands! He smashed right into a tree.

GUTTER CAT

Danny decided to take Hayley for a walk one day and she wanted me to come too. I didn't want go because I knew by the time we got back, my bad toe would be killing me. But she insisted, so I went.

On the way back, I was hurtin' pretty bad so I was behind them, trying to keep up.

Then Danny noticed a dead, black cat layin' in the gutter. Instead of ignoring it and blocking it from Hayley's view, he walked over to it. He thought it was our cat.

"Oh, no," he said to Hayley, "I think that's Spooky."

Hayley naturally started crying. Danny, wanting to give our treasured pet a proper burial, reached down and peeled the corpse off the street. Its head was all crushed, with its eyeballs hanging out. Seeing her beloved pet's poor face all mangled up made Hayley start wailing.

He carried it home; beer cup in one hand, dead cat danglin' from the other, hysterical kid losing her mind, and my fat ass hobblin' behind them. We were a sight.

We got back across the street from our house and were waiting for all the cars to go by when Hayley abruptly stopped crying and said, "Daddy look! There's Spooky!"

Our fuckin' cat was sitting on our porch.

THE UNFORTUNATE SNAKE

I was on the porch one afternoon, watching for Danny and the girls to come back from their walk. Here they came; Annie and Hayley out front, Danny bringing up the rear.

"Watch out!!!" I heard him scream, as he bolted between the girls. He reached down and picked up a live snake.

The poor thing was minding its own business, just trying to slither across their path. Instead of throwing the two-foot black snake in the bushes, like any sober man would do, drunk Danny ripped its fuckin' head off and dropped the pieces back on the sidewalk. The poor girls were traumatized.

FLOWERS

Danny took Hayley on a walk one Mother's Day so I could take a nap. I woke up to a huge, beautiful bouquet of flowers in a vase on the coffee table. There was every kind of flower you could think of, in every color of the rainbow. I was thrilled. The flower lady must have set up shop at the beer store, I thought.

"How much did you have to pay for those?" I asked. While appreciative, I knew we didn't have money for flowers - Danny was out of work again.

"They were free momma. Me and daddy picked them for you," little Hayley proudly beamed.

"Picked them from where?" I asked. I glanced at Danny and he was just looking at the ceiling.

"Out of all the neighbor's yards," she answered innocently.

The drunk idiot had taught our daughter how to steal.

Those weren't the only flowers he stole for me. Hydrangea bushes are my very favorite. Over the years, no matter how hard I tried, I couldn't grow one to save my life.

On one of my birthdays, he took me outside, around to the front side of my house. A huge, pink and blue hydrangea bush had magically appeared in my yard!

Danny had gotten wasted the night before and wanted to do something special for my birthday. So, in the middle of the night, he snuck into the neighbor's yard and dug up their bush and replanted it in ours. And he didn't even have the sense to plant it in the backyard where no one could see it.

PET MOUSE

Before we got a cat, we had a mouse problem. Annie could hear them skittering across her room, so we put some of those sticky, humane mousetraps in there.

Well, we caught one. It was still alive and just a little thing, so Danny carefully detached it from the glue, wrapped a tissue around it like a blanket, and for some fucked-up reason, gave it to our four-year old to hold.

I was in the other room when I heard my baby let out an ear piercing scream. I ran in there to find drunk Danny with the mouse in one hand, and Hayley's little hand in his other, tears running down her face. The fuckin' mouse had bit her.

LAWNMOWER MAN

Danny's favorite pastime was riding his lawnmower around the backyard with an ice cold beer in his hand. I guess it reminded him of the good ole days when was a drunk driver. He also like to have Hayley help him mow the grass. She'd sit in his lap and they'd ride around the yard.

One day I happened to glance out the window and saw Danny standing on the patio, but I also heard the lawn mower running. I looked out into the yard and to my holy horror, saw my six-year-old on the riding lawn mower cutting the grass all by herself. I about tripped over my feet trying to get out the back door.

"Danny," I screamed, "What the hell are you thinking? Get her off that thing!"

"It's okay," he said, "I turned the blade off; she's havin' fun driving."

"NOW" I screamed.

"Okay, okay," he mumbled, walking out into the yard.

"Hayley," he yelled, catching her eye, "momma says you have to stop."

Well, apparently the dumbass forgot to teach the kid how to stop and in her attempt, she changed gears and started going faster. I started screaming and about had a heart attack as I watched my baby panic and jump off the still in motion lawnmower. I ran to her as he ran to his favorite toy.

Trying his best to hop up on the run away mower, still with the beer cup in his hand, he tripped over himself, went down and the damn thing ran over his foot. While he was rolling around on the ground in pain, soaked in beer at this point, I watched the mower crash into the playhouse.

Buzz

The county was on us about the Bronco sitting in our driveway because it didn't have tags or stickers. They threatened to tow it if we didn't make it street legal, but since we didn't have any money for that, Danny decided he was gonna hide it in our backyard. But to get to our back yard, he would have to take down part of the neighbor's fence and drive it through their yard-which he did without asking them.

He asked Hayley if she wanted to ride with him, but since he had been drinking like always, I said no. I told her to wait on the back porch for him.

I went in the kitchen to do some dishes and watch through the window to see where he would park the piece of shit.

Here he came, chug chugin' into my back yard through the ten-foot gap he had made in the neighbor's fence. And he wonders why people hate us.

He started waving to Hayley and ran right into the railroad tie surrounding my flower garden. He backed up then stopped. I could see him in there waving his arms, then he jumped out.

He was dancing around yard like a fuckin' idiot, and I thought, "What the hell is wrong with him?"

43

Hayley ran over to him, then she started dancing around too and waving her arms. They started running towards the house and flew in the back door-followed by a swarm of fuckin' bees!

We were all screaming and swatting and getting stung until we could make it out the front door.

"What the hell happened?" I asked him.

There was a bee's nest hiding under the railroad tie the drunk shit ran over.

HE SHOULDN'T BITCH AT ME

We took another trip to Disney World. We flew this time and rented a car-I had learned my lesson about the Auto Train.

The year we went, the stink bug outbreak was really bad in Virginia. The little fuckers were everywhere and our house was infested. Lucky for us, Florida didn't have any.

After we got settled in our room, we all jumped in the rental car to go to Walmart to buy food for the week-God forbid we have any money to eat in restaurants. Danny had been drinking since he got on the plane, so he was drunk. Annie wanted to sit in the front seat, so I put Danny behind me, in the back with Hayley.

This was before I had a phone with GPS, so we had to go by the directions the front desk had given us. Since I ain't got no sense of direction, I got lost. Lost in Florida.

We were driving around, trying to find the Walmart, and Danny started bitchin' at me. He wanted more beer and he wanted it now.

"Sit back and smoke your cigarette," I told him, trying to figure out where the hell I was.

We weren't allowed to smoke in the rental car, so we both had our windows down to let the smoke escape.

He was back there goin' on and on, bitchin' me out for getting lost, whining for more beer. I couldn't concentrate with his big mouth running so much and got more lost.

All of a sudden, Annie started screaming. There was a stink bug crawlin' up her thigh; apparently the little fucker had hitched a ride in one of our suitcases and escaped when we weren't lookin'. Without thinking, I reached over, grabbed it and threw it out my window.

Half a second later, in the middle of his rant, Danny started choking.

When I threw the stinkbug out my window, the wind caught it and sailed it back in through his and it flew in his open bitchin' mouth and down his throat. Funniest goddamn thing I ever saw.

DOG SITTER

Every time we dog sat for someone, drunk Danny managed to turn it into chaos one way or another. He had no sense and all the alcohol only made his judgement worse.

When our lab Twinkie was about a year old, my ex-husband asked me to watch his lab, Woody, so he could go out of town for the weekend.

On Saturday, Danny decided to walk both dogs and both kids down to the park. When they got there, drunk Danny let Twinkie off the leash to run. There was a leash law, but he didn't give a shit.

Annie told him not to let Woody off his leash, but the dumbass did it anyway. I guess Woody decided he didn't want to live with us anymore. He took off and ran for the hills.

Annie came running in the door crying. She told me that Danny had lost Woody.

Now, how the hell was I supposed to tell my ex-husband I lost his damn dog?

One of Danny's friends needed us to watch her dog while she went on vacation. It was a big German Shepard named Coco. This friend of his had no children; the dog was her child.

She dropped Coco off with a large metal cage, a bag of expensive dog food and specific instructions that the dog was ONLY to eat the dog food. Coco had never eaten people food.

That night, we set up the cage in the corner and put the dog to bed.

The next morning, I went downstairs to make my coffee and an awful stink hit me. I followed my nose to the back room where Coco's cage was. The bottom of the cage was smeared with doggie diarrhea. The shit must have squirted out her ass while she was standing up cause it had shot through the cage and was all over my walls, too.

I went to wake Danny to tell him what had happened. Half asleep, he confessed that he had fed the dog his left over tacos from the night before. The fuckin' idiot!

My sister rescued a pug named George. It was the ugliest pug I ever saw. And it was old, which didn't help its looks. She loved that pitiful thing so much. She needed me to take care of it one weekend. I said sure, and promised her I would take very good care of him.

Three hours after she dropped him off, Danny came home from work. I asked him to let the dogs out. He went out with them. A little later, he came inside with Twinkie trailing behind him.

"Where's George?" I asked.

"Who the hell is George?" he answered.

"Oh my God! George is Summer's dog. Where is he?"

"In the back yard."

I went outside to get the Pug and the gate was wide open. George was gone.

Both lost dogs were eventually found, safe and sound, and Coco recovered.

Pussy Whipped

One day, Danny came home from work (he had found yet another job) and was playing with Spooky the cat. I don't know what the hell he did to her but she scratched him. This made drunk Danny mad, so he decided to clip her nails. This pissed her off more, so she bit him; hard.

The next day, his fuckin' hand had blown up like a balloon and was all infected so he couldn't go to work for days. Half the time I think the dumbass gets himself hurt on purpose just to get out of working.

HORSING AROUND

We were poor as dirt cause drunk man had lost another job and couldn't find a new one to save his fuckin' life. So, to pay the bills, I started a yard sale business in my yard trying to turn other people's trash into some treasure for me.

One day, one of my regular customers told me she had some stuff to sell. She was a little older than me and her name was Judy. She seemed like a looney bin, but I needed money so I made an appointment to go to her house the next day.

When I got there, she had some really cool stuff to sell and dollar signs appeared in my eyes. While we were outside looking at her yard items, she introduced me to her horse, Gerald. His name should have been "Geritol". I don't know how this thing was still alive. It was really old and looked like it could keel over at any time. I don't know what kind it was, but it wasn't as big as a normal horse. It could have been a donkey for all I knew.

We went back in the house and she started talking. And talking and talking. She told me lots of personal shit I didn't want to hear, but I wanted to sell her stuff, so I sat there and listened.

About three and half hours into our appointment, Danny called to find out where the hell I was. I said still at the appointment and made the mistake of mentioning the horse. Well, he wanted to bring the girls over to ride the damn horse. I figured if I let them come over, they could take a ride then I could get the hell out of there. Judy said it would be fabulous for the girls to take a ride.

Before I left to go get my family, Judy said we could stay for dinner. I didn't want to stay for dinner, but what the hell could I do? This crazy lady had adopted me as her new best friend and my kids were excited to ride the fuckin' horse. So I said okay.

They were all outside waiting for me; Danny with a six pack. I could tell he was already loaded, but I took him anyway. He liked to talk, especially when he was drunk, so he could talk to Judy for a while and give me a break.

She led us out to the horse stall and Danny and the kids met Gerald. The girls were 11 and 5 at the time, and this small, old horse was just their speed. Judy didn't have a saddle because Gerald wasn't a riding horse- which the fuckin' loon neglected to tell me until I had my whole family at her house and we were trapped. But Danny popped Annie up there anyway, bareback.

He was leading the horse around the pen and Annie was doing good; until he led them under a tree and his drunk mind misjudged the height of Annie on the horse and a big branch slapped her across the face and cut her. Of course, she started crying; her ride was over.

While I was dealing with Annie, Danny put Hayley on the horse. He was at least holding on to her as she rode, but with one hand because his other was holding his bottle of beer. He must have thought his five-year-old could handle riding on her own, because he let go of her and slapped the horse on its ass. This spooked poor old Gerald and he bucked. Hayley went flying off, and fell right into a pile of horse shit. She started screaming.

The stupid mother fucker; I should have left him at home.

After I calmed her down and cleaned her off, I said it was time to cook dinner and we all needed to go inside. Danny was having none of that. He had a horse to play with, and both kids wanted to stay outside. I made it very clear that he was not to put them back on the horse, then Judy and I went inside to fix dinner. She pulled some steaks out of the freezer and we started cooking.

Dinner was almost ready, so I went to retrieve my family. I walked out the door and what did I see? Fuckin' Danny was pouring his beer down Gerald's throat and the horse was just gulpin' away like it was in a chuggin' contest.

"Danny!" I screamed. He jumped and pulled the beer bottle away.

"What?" he said, guilt on his face, "he likes it."

"Get your ass in here," I hissed, looking back to make sure Judy hadn't seen the idiot trying to intoxicate her horse.

We ate dinner and I think it was the worst meal I had ever had. Those fuckin' steaks must have been in that freezer for twenty years. They were so tough; I couldn't even chew mine. I ended up hiding most of my steak in my napkin and throwing it away. Thank God I had brought Spaghetti O's for the kids or they might have choked to death. It appeared Danny had eaten his, his fake teeth serving him well.

I started to help clear the table and Danny said he was taking the girls back out to see Gerald. I said no; it was getting late and I didn't want them outside. I had spent most of the day with this crazy bitch and wanted to go home. He fought me on it, and Judy backed him up, so out they went.

When everything was clean, I saw my escape. I gathered my stuff and thanked her for dinner. I told her I would call her to set a time to start working; then we heard the yelling. We ran into the foyer as Annie came in shouting that Gerald was loose.

We hurried to the front porch just in time to see Danny chasing the horse around the property. The damn thing was sprier than I thought it ever could be. Danny couldn't catch it and he fell down twice. Judy was yelling and her face looked stricken. The next thing I knew, Gerald was heading for the open gate. Then he was gone!

Judy screamed for me to call 911.

"For a *horse*?" I asked, in disbelief.

"Yes! Call them NOW!" she screamed and took off, Danny running after her.

Well, I didn't know if you were allowed to call 911 for a fuckin' horse and I didn't want to get in trouble, so I called the nonemergency police line. I was scared not to call somebody; this crazy bitch was losin' it.

The cop didn't seem too interested, but said he would call animal control and send them out. I didn't feel comfortable being in her house alone, so the girls and I went out on the porch to wait.

About an hour later, Danny came stumbling back to the house, out of breath.

"Did ya find it?" I asked.

"No", he said, "we were in a field and that bitch told me to sit down."

"What?"

"She made me sit in the fuckin' field. She said she didn't need my help; I had done enough."

"So what did you do?"

"I sat down."

"How did it get out in the first place?" I asked.

"I told Annie to close the gate."

I looked at Annie; she was looking at Danny like he was crazy with her mouth hanging open. Well, shit. What were we supposed to do now? Judy was nowhere in sight. The four of us were just sitting on her porch. Danny was bitchin' because she made him sit in a field. If the damn horse got hit by a car, I didn't know what was gonna happen to us. I was so mad at him. He was blaming Annie. I was blaming him because I told him not to go back outside. It was getting later and later; still no Gerald or Judy.

We waited a while longer, then Danny said we were leaving; he needed another beer. I left her a note, drove around for a while searching for the horse, then went home and worried all night. Needless to say, I didn't get to sell her stuff. Gerald had found a field of crops and almost ate itself to death. Judy had to call in an emergency vet in the middle of the night.

If fuckin' people would listen to me, bad shit wouldn't happen!

THE NAME GAME

Before the alcohol took total control and Danny earned the nicknames "asshole", "loser", "moron", "drunk shit", and "fucker", he had other, nicer nicknames.

One day he was shoveling heavy, wet snow and threw his back out. He had to walk around half bent over for a week and of course, couldn't go to work. We started calling him "Broke Back Danny".

Annie's dad and his new family were over at our house for a cookout. Annie's stepbrother wanted to throw the football around. Her dad didn't want to play at the time, so drunk Danny volunteered.

He was running around the backyard showing off, and his foot went into a gopher hole. He went down screaming. He had jammed his damn toe. He was then referred to as "Sausage Toe".

It was the night before one of my yard sales, so I put everyone in the car to go put up the signs. Since I had to drive, Danny would hop out and staple gun the posters to street signs.

I saw a street sign that was about twelve feet from the road, not usually where I would put one, but pulled over anyway. Danny gathered his supplies and got out of the car. I was watching him go, but turned my head for a second. When I looked back, he was gone!

"Where'd daddy go?" I asked the girls. We looked all around, but didn't see him. Then he magically reappeared! He was hobbling back to the car and I noticed my damn sign wasn't up.

"Where were you?" I asked.

"I fell in a fuckin' ditch!" he said.

Apparently, just before the street sign, there was a five-foot deep ditch in the ground. It was dark, and he was drunk, so he didn't see it. He was just moseying along and "oops!" he fell in the hole.

I told him to get back over there and put my sign up. He didn't want to, but I made him.

He said, "Ok, but I'm gonna show you how deep that thing is. I really hurt myself!"

So we all watched. He was limping back; then all we could see was his head sticking out of the ground giving us a dirty look. We thought this was hilarious. We saw him climb out the other side and put the sign up, then fall back in the ditch and climb out our side. We were still laughing as he got into the car.

His new name was "Ditch Daddy."

THE METRO TRAIN

He lost the job at the dealership that was a quick bus ride from home. I can't remember if he got fired or got mad and quit; there were so many I couldn't keep track. But, he didn't have a goddamn job no more. I was back on Craigslist, job searching for him. He didn't have a clue how to use a computer (or a cell phone, or a TV remote control) and had no desire to learn. For God's sake, up until 2015 when I said I didn't know something, he told me to go "Ask Jeeves".

Finding a new job for him wasn't easy; he had burnt bridges all over northern Virginia. There were some places he hadn't worked at yet, but they required a driver's license, which he still didn't have cause it costs a lot of money to get your driver's license back after you act like a fuckin' moron too many times and get branded a habitual offender.

He found a job a few weeks later in bum-fuck Maryland. It cost a fortune to tow his tool box there. Have I mentioned his damn tool box before? It's bigger than a Smart Car and weighs a ton. You can't just throw it in the back of a pickup truck; it has to be towed on a flatbed tow truck which has cost us up to $500. Sometimes it only costs $200 to move, but when you're moving that bitch two to three times a year, that shit adds up.

I've begged him to downsize to a regular toolbox to make it easier and cheaper to move, but he won't do it. He says it's a "prestige" thing. Yeah buddy; so is having a fuckin' job.

He was working in Maryland, which meant he had to take the bus to the metro station, ride the train, then take another bus to the job. It took him forever to get there and forever to get home. I was okay with that. I only had to put up with his shit for a few minutes in the morning and about an hour at night, and then on the weekends (most of which he slept away cause he was always hung over).

I was upstairs cleaning one morning and heard the front door open. When I didn't hear my named called, I knew what was coming. Danny didn't go to work; or he did, and got fired-AGAIN! "Shit," I thought, here we go again. "Why couldn't he just be normal?"

I walked down the stairs and was shocked. Danny's shirt was covered in blood. There was a bloody rag wrapped around his arm and his face was all fucked up.

"What happened to you?" I asked.

"I got mugged on the metro."

"Are you alright?" I asked, not sure if I really cared or not.

"Do I look alright, Dawn?" he said in a tone I didn't appreciate; like it was my fault because I made the fucker go to work.

"Well, did you call the police and report it?"

"No. I don't want anything to do with cops," he stated.

"Well, did you at least report it to the metro? They have cameras on those trains, don't they?"

"No, they won't do anything," he said, and then started taking selfie pictures of his wounds.

"If you're not calling the cops, why are you taking pictures?"

"For my boss."

Dammit; he was gonna milk this one for all it was worth and take more time off work.

RODENTS

Our house was slowly turning into a zoo. Spooky the cat turned out to be a whore and was having kittens every six months. I know I should have gotten her fixed, but we couldn't afford the vet bill.

Hayley managed to con me into keeping one kitten from each litter. I turned them all into outdoor cats.

Twinkie, Spooky and the various kittens weren't enough for her though; she wanted a guinea pig. I thought of guinea pigs as big hamsters and told her okay. I had no money to buy the kid expensive toys or electronics, the least I could do was let her have pets.

We went to the pet store and I almost shit when I found out a stupid guinea pig was $32.00 and the cage was almost $50. That didn't even count the ball to roll around the floor in, the wheel or the food. I had to break my baby's heart, but we just weren't in the position to spend that kind of money; drunk ass had been fired again.

I was at a school fundraiser one day and there was a woman there trying to get rid of her two guinea pigs. I said my daughter wanted a guinea pig, and she was more than happy to hand hers over. I could also have the cage and the food; for free! This sounded good to me; if it's free, it's for me!

She told me how sweet and loving they were and how they would talk to each other. I was excited to surprise Hayley, so, after the event, I followed the lady to her house to pick them up.

I soon found out that I did not like guinea pigs. All they did was shit and make noise. But, Hayley loved them, so we kept them.

One night, drunk Danny woke Hayley up at 3 am.

"Hey! Hey!" he said while nudging her side. "Your guinea pigs are hungry; you want to feed them?"

My little girl peeled open her eyes and said, "Ok," and got out of bed.

They went downstairs and Hayley went to get the carrots from the fridge. When she came back, her father was feeding one of them beer through a straw! Its little jaws were really working it.

Hayley screamed, "Dad! What are you doing?"

He said, "Oh, I've been doing this for an hour. He likes it."

Then he put the guinea pig down on the floor. The poor thing started running around in circles and then BAM; it crashed right into the coffee table.

Danny yelled, "Oh no, it's got a load!" Now, we don't know what that meant, but Hayley started laughing hysterically.

I came to hate the guinea pigs. They were filthy, loud animals. When they kept biting Hayley, I convinced her they needed to go.

She said, "Could I have a hamster instead?" I said yes, thinking that a hamster wouldn't be any trouble. I was also living in the 1970's and thought I could buy one for fifty cents.

We tried to find the guinea pigs a new home. We asked everyone we knew if they would take them. They all said, "Hell no". They were smarter people than I was. So we decided to take them to the animal shelter. Danny, me and Hayley packed them in the car and we were on our way.

As soon as we pulled into the parking lot, Hayley started crying. Shit! I calmed her down by reminding her she was going to get a cute little hamster that she could hold and love.

I told Danny to go ahead and take them in.

"Why do I have to do it?" he asked, appalled that I would make him turn over his drinking buddies.

"I can't lift the cage and it would be too hard for Hayley if we all went in," I reasoned.

So, in he went.

When he came out, he was mad as hell. They gave him a really hard time, and made him feel like shit. The lady even started crying. Then she made him fill out a form. Danny is not good at filling out forms; at all. He was so discombobulated from the lady putting him on a guilt trip and trying to fill out the form, he wrote down the wrong names for the pigs, and couldn't remember our address. Maybe he should have asked Jeeves.

POOR LITTLE HAMSTERS

Over the years, many hamsters have called our house home; unfortunately for them.

Our first hamsters were sisters we named Alice and Rosalie (I actually named them-my kindred spirits will get the reference.) One day, Hayley went to go check on them. Rosalie was laying in her food bowl. Hayley lifted her up and her neck was poking out every which way. Apparently she was stuffing her face, choked, and died. Hayley screamed and Danny came running.

"My hamster's dead," Hayley cried.

"It's not dead; I can fix it," Danny slurred.

As Hayley was checking Alice, she heard thumping. She turned to see her father pounding on Rosalie's chest with his fist, trying to bring it back to life.

Hayley said, "Well, it's dead now."

Our cat, Spooky, who happened to be a polydactyl, had found out there was live food within reach.

One day, Danny saw her walking down the hall with something in her mouth. It was Alice. While the cat hadn't hurt her yet, Spooky acquired a taste for hamster.

She figured out how to open the cage with help from her extra claws. She got in there another day and pulled Alice out. Playing with her before the kill, the cat ripped her open all the way from her little chest to her tiny hamster knee. Before eating her, she lost interest and left Alice for dead.

Hayley came home from school and found the hamster laying on the floor. It looked dead to her. She didn't want to touch it, and neither did I, so we left it for Danny. He got home and apparently the hamster was just in shock, so he put it back in the cage.

A couple of nights later, drunk Danny called Hayley over and said, "Hey Hayley, your hamster's awake; you wanna play?"

Well, Hayley had forgotten about the injury because she was just a little kid. She said, "Okay."

Danny forgot about the injury too because he was a drunk. He reached in the cage, grabbed the hamster, and while doing so, his pinky slid into the open wound. It freaked him out so much, he flung it towards the ceiling. It hit the ceiling fan and bounced on the bed. Hayley screamed and ran to save it. Thank God, it lived to see another day.

Hayley liked to teach her hamsters how to climb the stairs by themselves. One day, she was giving Alice her lesson when Danny appeared. He wanted to help.

We have an open staircase, and Alice poked her head out through the railings halfway up the stairs. Danny decided to pat her on the butt; like he did that damn horse. This frightened the poor little thing and she jumped.

"Look Hayley, your hamster can fly," said Danny as Alice flew through the air.

We moved her cage down to the living room and put it on top of a hutch where the cat couldn't get it. Danny came across another hamster cage mixed in with our junk and decided to make the hamster a homemade Habitrail.

He didn't do a very good job connecting the cages, and eventually Alice escaped. She fell to the floor with a loud thump, alerting the cat. Spooky pounced on her and started batting her around.

Danny walked in and saw what was happening. He scooped Alice up, but she wasn't breathing. Any normal person would have it in a box and let their kid have a funeral for it. Not drunk Danny. He knew Hayley loved the thing, so he did the only thing he could think of: he gave it mouth to mouth resuscitation and brought it back to life.

Our next hamster was Butterball, who was very sweet and never bit. Drunk Danny decided that Butterball might like to help him mow the lawn. Calm down; he didn't run over her with the lawn mower, although that easily could've happened.

Hayley looked out the window and saw her hamster on her father's shoulder as he was trying to start the lawn mower. She ran outside just in time to see her precious hamster fall off and hit the ground.

Free at last, it took off running. Not knowing where the hell it was, it bee-lined right into a pile of dog shit and got stuck. Hayley was pissed!

Butterball had been living in Hayley's bedroom, and one day, I decided she needed a change of scenery. I brought the cage down to the living room so she could be around all of us and have new things to look at. We had learned our lesson concerning the cat, so the hamster now lived safely in a glass aquarium.

One night, Annie's boyfriend said, "What's wrong with that hamster?"

We all looked, and she was running madly on her wheel, banging her head into the side of it. I asked Danny if he had fed her beer. He said no. I wasn't convinced.

A couple of days later, Hayley went to feed her and she was dead. Her poor little stomach was ripped wide open. She had committed suicide. I guess looking at drunk Danny all the time was just too much for her. I feel her pain.

A month or so later, Hayley started begging for another hamster.

"Please, baby, no. They all die and you get so upset," I pleaded.

But she wouldn't stop begging, so I finally said okay. She wanted to try a different pet store. Her friend had bought one in Winchester, and it lived a long time, so we went there.

Winchester happens to be where our favorite restaurant in the whole world is. The Golden Corral! It's forty minutes from home, so we don't go there a lot. Plus, we can't afford to go there a lot cause Danny would rather drink and watch fifty year old movies than work.

I figured if we were in town buying another fuckin' hamster, we might as well have dinner there. Hayley wanted to eat first, so we wouldn't have to leave the new hamster in the car, but the pet store was closing soon.

We named this one Smokey. Smokey came in a cardboard house with a handle on it.

We got to the restaurant and Hayley wanted to bring the damn thing in with us. She said it was too cold to leave it outside. It wasn't that cold; and the thing had fur.

Then she said she was afraid it would get out of the box. I made sure the box was securely closed, and made her leave it in the car.

We got back in the dark car and Hayley looked in the box. The fuckin' hamster had chewed a hole right through the cardboard and was loose in the car somewhere. My car is a dumpster on wheels so I didn't know how the hell we were gonna find that thing, especially at night, but knew there was enough old French-fries on the floor to feed it for a month.

Hayley was crying, so I promised her we'd find it when we got home. Danny was bitching that it probably went under the dash and was chewing the wires. I was in a food coma and trying not to wreak the car.

All of a sudden, Danny jumped and said the hamster just ran over his foot. He stuck his hand down there and grabbed it. Then she bit him, so he let go.

Hayley was screaming for her hamster. Danny took his seatbelt off and turned his big ass around so that his head was in the foot well and his feet were in the air. He was rummaging through all the trash on the floor and found her when she bit him again.

Danny, The Maid From Hell

We're not the cleanest people in the world. The five-second rule doesn't apply here-you'd get fuckin' ptomaine poison if you ate off our floor. All Danny really liked to do was ride around the yard on the lawnmower while consuming a six pack, or blow all the leaves out into the busy street so when cars drove by the wind would catch them and they would settle in our neighbor's yards-that way he didn't have to bag them.

But sometimes he did get ambitious and try to help clean the house. Which was really no help at all cause the only time the urge to clean hit him, he was drunk and created more work for me.

When he tried to dust, he'd drop things and they'd break. His version of vacuuming consisted of taking a t-shirt and slapping it against the floor so that all the dog hair, dust and dirt would fly into the air and land somewhere else. Instead of using a mop to clean the kitchen floor, he would throw boiling water all over the place, take my good bath towels, stand on them and scoot his ass around the room.

None of that compared to the time he got really creative. The main level looked like a tornado had swept through. I was upstairs getting the laundry together when I heard a noise that sounded like the vacuum cleaner but not exactly. I came downstairs to find him in my living room with the fuckin' leaf blower, blowing everything that was light enough towards the front door. What the idiot didn't realize was that dirt from the outdoors (because he never put anything away) was flying out the return vent on the blower, covering everything in his wake.

How Dumb Could He Be?

Danny got home from work one day with a pissed off look on his face.

"You're gonna have to drive me to and from work for a few days; until things calm down," he said.

"Why?" I asked, dreading the answer; this was Danny after all.

"Bitch threw me off the bus."

"Did they catch you drinking?" I sighed.

Danny always drank beer on the bus cause he couldn't wait five fuckin' minutes to get home and do it.

"No, they caught me smoking in the bathroom."

"Why in the hell would you smoke on a bus?" I asked. What a fuckin' moron!

"I don't know, Dawn; I wanted to," he answered with an attitude.

"How did you get caught? Did somebody smell it and report you?"

"No, alarms started going off. I flushed my beer and when I walked out, she had pulled over on the toll road and told me the cops were on their way."

"For God's sake! Did you get arrested?"

"No, but they told me I was banned from the bus then left me on the side of the road. I had to hitchhike home."

"Well, that's just fuckin' great. I don't have enough to do, now I have to spend two hours a day driving you."

"I'm sorry! I didn't think I'd get caught," he said.

"That's because you can't think at all. Your brain is so saturated with alcohol, you do fucked-up things."

"And you're just perfect."

"I'm not a fuckin' idiot!"

"I'm not gonna fight with you," he said and walked to the fridge.

I sat there looking after him, shaking my head. What the hell was wrong with him? Was he really that stupid, or was he sabotaging himself, trying to get out of going to work because he knew damn well the last thing I wanted to do was drive his ass?

My Odd Jobs

It was getting harder and harder for him to keep a job, then harder for him to find a new one cause he was a fuckin' raging alcoholic. We were going deeper and deeper into debt and it was all we could do to make the minimum payments on the credit cards. Homeboy was content to numb himself with alcohol so he didn't have to worry about it.

The town had shut down my yard sale business cause apparently you were only allowed to have two yard sales a year without a peddler's license. I rented a booth in a second hand shop to sell my junk and put some of it on Ebay, but that wasn't making enough and we needed some fuckin' health insurance. I started taking any work I could get.

I took a temp job as a hostess at a new homes development. That was interesting. I had to dress up and look somewhat like a Realtor, which was hard; I had to dig deep into my closet. The first day I worked, I wore a pheasant skirt from the eighties-it was the best I could do.

The new homes were townhouses with long staircases to the front doors. A nice looking couple came in and we headed over to the models to take a look. On the short walk over, the elastic in my ten-year old panties broke.

I could feel them slipping on the short walk over, and while I was trying my hardest to walk with my legs together, they were almost to my knees by the time we reached the house. I knew if I tried to climb the stairs before my customers, my raggedy ass briefs would be around my ankles and trip me, crashing me back down the stairs on top of the people.

I presented the stairs and said "after you." As soon as their backs were turned, I reached down inside my skirt and yanked my panties back up as high as they would go and held on till they left.

The next weekend I wore pants. A couple came in that didn't look like they could afford a mortgage, but what do I know? I was poor as a fuckin' church mouse and still managed to pay mine. I showed them the models and they were interested.

We sat at the conference table and they filled out a financial sheet. Checking to make sure all the blanks were filled, I saw that they worked for a funeral home. I asked them what their positions were and they told me transport. I asked them what that was even though I thought I knew.

"We drive the dead bodies from the hospital to the funeral home," the wife said.

I guess I got a funny look on my face because then the husband informed me they were on a job as we spoke.

"You mean you're transporting a dead body now?"

"Yeah, two of them. You wanna see?"

Well, I thought he was just yanking my chain so I said yes. We walked out to their station wagon and I peaked in the window. The backseats had been folded down and there were two body bags laying there. I was still doubtful about what I was seeing, so he opened the back door and unzipped a bag. He slung it open and there was a dead guy in all his naked glory. They asked me if I wanted to see the woman, but I had seen enough.

It didn't occur to me until later that it was strange the people were driving a beat up old station wagon filled with dead bodies instead of a vehicle with the funeral home's name on it. For all I know, they could have murdered those people and stole their identities.

I got a part-time job as a bookkeeper for a veterinary surgeon, which I love. I was hired at twenty hours a week, but once I figured out what I was doing, it only took me five hours a week. I still needed more; and insurance.

THE BIG YELLOW SCHOOL BUS

I thought driving a school bus would be a good job for me. The schedule worked, the pay was very good and the county health insurance rocked. A dream job, right? Wrong.

Worse fuckin' job I ever had! Let me tell you, driving a school bus ain't no joke! I thought I would just give the same kids a ride every day; just like driving my own kids. It didn't work out that way.

The training part was okay. I spent two weeks in a classroom and got paid very well for sitting there. I learned first aid and got certified in CPR.

I learned about the special needs buses. I didn't want to drive those; I was too scared. I thought I would fuck up trying to load a kid in a wheelchair or something.

They told us not to cuss at the kids; that it would be very bad if we did. Well, that was gonna be a problem. Cuss words spilled out of my mouth without me even knowing it.

They showed us an example of a route sheet. It had directions of where we were supposed to pick-up and drop-off each kid. This would be an even greater challenge for me than controlling my mouth. The majority of the routes did not have "bus stops" because we were in rural country. Buses stopped at each kid's house. Even though I wore glasses for distance, I still couldn't see street signs that well. And because they were for distance, anything I tried to read up close was just a blur, so I would have to move my glasses to read each address. But, optimist me thought, "I'll just learn the route in a week and then I'll be okay." I was wrong again.

They didn't just give you a route of your own right off the bat. You had to be a substitute first, which meant they could put me on any damn route they wanted to. Every day I worked was a fuckin' nightmare. Not only did I never know where the hell I was, I couldn't drive the forty -four-foot death trap in reverse worth a damn-especially with up to fifty rowdy kids sitting behind me. I didn't actually make a turn in reverse without hitting a cone until I was taking the test. And that was after three tries. They must have been really hard up for drivers; I still can't believe they gave me permission to drive a bunch of kids around.

After I got my license paperwork, they took me into the dispatch center to meet the people that would be calling me with assignments. A very nice man told me he had an opening for the next day. It was on a special needs bus. My stomach tightened, but he was so nice and I didn't want to seem unappreciative, so I said okay.

The only thing that seemed good about the special needs bus was that there was an attendant on board. She would take care of the kids while I drove. She would also help me with the directions.

The attendants were always very nice and told me where to turn. I only had to load a wheelchair once, and the attendant helped me, so I didn't fuck it up. Most of the special needs buses were also a lot shorter, so that helped.

Turned out, special needs buses were the only buses I enjoyed driving; but those jobs came few and far between. The rest of it was a living hell.

Driving the regular kids on the big buses was a fuckin' nightmare I couldn't wake up from. Every goddamn day it was something. I still don't know how I didn't give myself a heart attack; it stressed me out so much.

It wasn't the kids that was the problem. I loved the kids. I was so busy trying to figure out where the hell I was and tryin' not to hit something, I let them do pretty much what they wanted. They loved me.

The first time I had to drive alone, it was an afternoon route. I pulled into the school and parked. Then I was told by an irate bus driver that I parked in the wrong damn place. Unbeknown to me, there is an order as to who you park in front of and who you park behind; how else are the kids gonna find their fuckin' bus? So I moved my bus.

The bell rang and all these cute little kids got on. They all wanted to know who I was and what was wrong with their regular driver. I told them, and also said I was new and asked if they wanted to help me find my way. They were all very eager to help, but not one of the little fuckers knew how to get to their house. I was gonna have to read directions; please God, help me.

We left the school and made a right turn. I read where the next turn was, but unlike MapQuest, the route sheet didn't tell me how many miles away it was. There was no GPS on the bus and I couldn't use the one on my phone. I was totally screwed; I'd have to read each street sign.

I was to turn on Smith Drive. Well, the kids were all talking to me at once and I was trying to be polite and talk back, and didn't see the sign until I was right on top of it, going 45 mph.

"Shit!!!" I shouted without thinking.

"Oooooooooooo. You said a bad word," they all chorused from behind me.

"Mother fuck," I thought, "They're bound to tell their parents and I'm gonna get fired!"

"I'm sorry," I said, "Please don't tell on me. I missed the turn."

I was desperately looking for a place to turn around when heaven sent me a miracle. Smith Drive was actually a circle and I could pick it up at the second entrance. "Thank you, Lord!"

I dropped that kid off and asked who was next. A little girl moved up to a front seat. Looking at my route sheet, I saw that she lived on the main road.

I said, "Okay honey, you think you can help me find your house?"

She said yes. But she couldn't. All she knew, was that it was a brown house and you couldn't see it from the road. I would have to drive slow to read the mailboxes. Another thing about this rural land: the fuckin' mailbox numbers don't go in order! They were all over the place. My heart was pounding, knowing if I flew past her house it was gonna be a bitch to turn around. Thank God a fifth grade boy knew the route and spoke up.

One day, I got a call for an afternoon route in the town right next to mine. I knew those roads well and was happy to take the job. When I asked for the bus number, dispatch told me I would need to use a spare bus; the driver I was subbing for kept her bus at home. All I needed to do, was go into the garage and tell the guy at the desk what route I had.

Okay, no problem, it will be an easy day.

I must be cursed, because I was fuckin' wrong again! Danny's black shit cloud had followed me to work.

I found the guy in the garage and told him what I needed. He started laughing and handed me the keys and a piece of paper with the bus number on it to tape on the door. I didn't know why this old fuck was laughing until I arrived at my bus.

There are two types of buses-regular ones and transit ones. The transit buses are the ones with the flat front and the front tires are behind the driver's seat. They suck.

First of all, this one was a transit bus. I hadn't driven one of those on my own yet. Next, it was old as dirt and looked like a prison bus. I did my inspection, then got on and started adjusting my mirrors. Let me tell you about the goddamn mirrors on buses; you know; the ones you need in order to see where the ass end of the bus is.

Those mirrors that stick out in the front are rounded so you can see if any kids are behind you. They give you a wide angled, distorted view, but that's okay; if you see movement, you just don't move. The mirrors on the side of the bus, on the other hand, are flat and very, very important; they should give you a clear view of your back tires so you don't run over anything.

This fuckin' bus had rounded mirrors out front and rounded mirrors on the side, distorting my rear view of everything!

So, I had my front tires behind me, and couldn't see exactly where my rear tires were going. I wanted to run, but time was a wastin' and I was supposed to be at the school. At least I knew where the hell I was going that day.

My bus was packed to capacity with elementary students. They were hootin' and hollarin', but I didn't care; I was just trying to remember where my front tires were.

As we pulled out of the pickup area, the bus lurched up, then crashed down. I saw the kids pop out of their seats in my mirror and some of them let out a scream.

I was so confused, I looked at the kid behind me and asked, "Did I a pothole?"

"It was the curb," his smart aleck mouth drawled.

Well, "fuck you" I wanted to say. He was looking at me like I was a moron, and I didn't appreciate his attitude.

That bus was a piece of shit. I hit curb after curb, because I just couldn't judge where the tires were in those fucked-up mirrors.

I got to a traffic light and had to make a right turn. The street was narrow and there was no way I was gonna make that turn without taking out half the sidewalk and a fire hydrant.

God Bless the man in the oncoming lane. He saw I wasn't gonna make it and backed up. With the use of his lane, I safely made the turn without destroying any public property. But, that kid was right, I did indeed look like a fuckin' moron.

I had had enough trouble with the afternoon routes, I didn't want any morning routes. One morning when the phone rang, instead of ignoring it like I usually did, my dumbass answered it.

They had a route for me. Against my better judgement, I accepted it. The route sheet was on the bus, she told me, and I needed to be at the first house in an hour.

I woke Danny up and told him he would have to take an earlier bus because I had to go to work. He wasn't happy, but he also wasn't supporting us, so I told him to get his ass ready. I woke the girls and told them they had to catch their bus on their own today.

When I got to my bus, the sun was just coming up, so at least I wouldn't have to find the kids in the dark. I did my safety checklist, found the route sheet and was on my way.

This route was in a town I was not familiar with at all, but I figured if I could just find the first kid, they could help me find the rest.

I managed to find the first house on my route and saw the kid and his mom in the driveway. I gave a sigh of relief. With a huge, friendly smile on my face, I waved to the mom through my open window and to my holy horror, heard her say, "That's okay, I'll take him." Then the bitch waved me away.

I followed the directions and made a turn down a one lane dirt road looking for the next kid. I started reading mailbox numbers and guess what? The fuckin' numbers didn't go in order. I was kicking myself in the ass for answering that damn phone!

The road was full of potholes, so I had to drive slowly. I carefully read each mailbox comparing the numbers to the sheet, while on the lookout for a kid or at least an open front door.

For the life of me, I couldn't find the house and there wasn't a soul in site. Next thing I knew, I reached the end of the road. With no time to turn the big rig around and start over, I checked the sheet and made the next turn. That kid must be out sick today or he would be outside, right? Wrong, again!

I found the rest of the kids and we were on the last leg of our journey when I heard someone calling my name through the CB radio.

"This is dispatch," a nice voice said. "Did you stop at 243 Elm Street?"

Oh shit! That must have been that kid I couldn't find! I lied and told her I did.

"Find a safe place, pull over and sit tight," said her once nice voice that now sounded irritated with me.

"Okay," I said. Dammit, now I was in trouble. Why did I have to pull over? The kids were gonna be late for school.

I found out why about ten minutes later when another school bus pulled up next to me and turned on its lights. I watched as a little boy got off and walked around to my door. I opened my door and as he boarded, he looked at me and said, "You forgot me," in a disgusted tone. Guess his mom didn't want to drive him, but the little bastard should've been waiting for me.

I never answered another morning call again. I wanted to wring Danny's drunk ass neck for making me go through this.

Another day, I was back on a regular bus with the wheels in front of me. I didn't know where I was going, but at least I could avoid the curbs.

The first few elementary kids lived in the country, so I had trouble finding their homes; but then I turned into a new, fancy neighborhood with street signs and mailbox numbers that went in order.

"Thank you, dear Jesus!" I praised. But he must not have heard me.

I easily found the first few houses, then checked my route sheet. I saw "TA" and cringed. I hated "TA's"; they meant "turn around" the 44-foot bus. "Fuck me!", I silently thought and headed to the intersection I was to "TA" at.

"Oh, no." I winced when I saw it. It was a "T" intersection. Some are simple; some are not. This one was not.

If you're driving up the vertical line of the "T", you simply turn one way or the other, back straight up, then turn forward to go back down the vertical line. Easy as pie! But if you're driving down the horizontal part of the "T", you desperately need to know how to make a turn in reverse-the ones I sucked at.

I pulled the bus up past the vertical "T" road; far enough, I thought, and threw the big bitch in reverse. I started the turn, missing the stop sign, looked in the other mirror and hit the brake. The left rear end was heading straight for the street sign. So, I pulled up and tried again.

First, I pulled straight back to get a better look of how far I should pull up to make the turn. Even if I missed the street sign, I still couldn't go into the grass because the grass was a ditch; a deep one like the one "Ditch Daddy" fell in.

If I fucked up, they would need a tow truck to get me out. I would have to cut the wheel as hard as could, and squeeze between the street sign and the stop sign.

After three more tries, I thought "Fuck It!"; I'm just gonna drive till I find a place that works for me."

I had to explain to the kids what I was doing; they were concerned the little old fat lady was kidnapping them. One of the little, rich bastards even had his cellphone out ready to dial 911.

I drove a little way, then I saw a man and his kid taking a walk. Stopping the bus, I opened the window.

"Excuse me," I yelled over the sound of the engine. "Is there any where I can turn this bus around by driving forward?"

Laughing at me, he said, "No, but there's a big cul-de-sac up there where you can turn around."

Breathing a sigh of relief, I thanked him and drove forward.

The cul-de-sac was free of vehicles, but not as big as I'd hoped. Scanning the area, I glazed over the tricycle in the street when I saw a large driveway leading to a big electrical box. Thanking the Lord in heaven, I started my turn around in that driveway, thinking the only thing I might hit was a curb.

When my bus was headed in the right direction, I glanced to my left and almost shit my pants. Somehow, that cute little tricycle was now in pieces!

"I couldn't have done that," I stupidly thought; "I didn't feel or hear anything. But, I must have; it was in one piece a minute ago. Dammit!"

I hauled ass out of that cul-de-sac before the kids could see it, or before some pissed off mom came running out her door.

Free of the cul-de-sac and thinking I was safe, I headed back from whence I came. Then I almost shit my pants again. I was coming back up to that intersection where I was supposed to "TA". The fuckin' street sign pole was now leaning halfway to the ground. In all my attempts to back in, I must have run over the mother fucker without knowing it. I was learning that nothing 44 feet behind me was registering in my brain. Now, I knew I was gonna get fired. I fucked up public property and the tricycle I ran over probably belonged to that nice man that helped me with directions, and he had seen my face.

I cussed Danny in my head all the way home. If the fucker was normal, I wouldn't have to go through this shit every day. My stomach was in knots by the time I got home, but, by the grace of God, I never heard a thing from my bosses about the damage I caused.

After taking a week off for my nerves to calm, I accepted a middle/high school route. I didn't know the streets, but the kids did. This day was actually fun. With a kid who was well versed on this route telling me where to go, I drove out to the country. They all lived on dirt roads that happened to be covered with potholes. With no way in hell of avoiding the craters, I just plowed through them.

This was an older bus and something was apparently wrong with my seat, because every hole I hit, popped me up in the air. The spring underneath must have been loose. It was like a grown-up Johnny Jumper seat. The deeper the hole, the higher I went. If I didn't have a seatbelt on, I would have bumped my head on the ceiling.

I still don't know why, maybe because I was feeling no stress, but every time I popped up, I started laughing hysterically. The kids were looking at me like I was crazy, and holding on for dear life because their seats didn't have seatbelts. Seeing them pop up in my overhead mirror made me laugh even harder. If my boss had watched the video that was taping me, I would've been fired for drinking on the job because I must have looked drunk.

My boss did think I was drunk one time. I wasn't, of course, I was just being me in a job I wasn't qualified to do. I had gotten to my bus and there was no route sheet. I called dispatch and they told me to go to the elementary school and someone would bring me my sheet.

I was at the school waiting, when I saw my boss coming. For some unknown reason, she waved for me to come out. When the bus isn't running, which mine wasn't, you can't open the door the regular way; you have to flip a certain switch, then it opens.

Well, I could never get all those fuckin' switches straight; it was like an airplane dashboard for God's sake. I was standing next to the door steps, flipping switches, and I don't know which one I hit, but it was definitely the wrong one! The damn bus started rolling and I almost fell into the stairwell! I jumped back in my seat and hit the brake before I hit the bus in front of me.

I looked out the door and there she was, wide eyed and very concerned. I was freaking out. I couldn't figure out how to open the door for my boss without the bus rolling away. Not knowing what else to do, I put my seatbelt on and started the bus. I opened the door the way I knew how, and she stepped on board.

She came right up close to me and asked skeptically, "Are you alright?"

I know she was checking to see if she could smell alcohol on my breath.

She wasn't the only boss that thought something was wrong with me. I had finished an elementary run with just enough time to get to the middle school. Problem was, I had to pee. I had to pee bad. There was no way I could wait an hour to deliver these kids and get back to the bus depot.

The closer I got to the school, the worse it got. I really was seriously terrified that my bladder was gonna burst and the kids were gonna have to step in pee to get to their seats.

We weren't allowed to leave our bus when kids were on it, but I had no choice. I had unbuttoned my pants so my bladder wasn't so squeezed, but it wasn't working; that pee was coming out any second. I pulled up and took my parking place.

The principle was standing at the school, holding the kids back until all the buses were stopped. I threw my bus into park, opened the door and grabbed the keys. Jumping off the bottom step, I saw the principle drop his arms and it was like racehorse gates had opened. Herds of kids were plowing towards me, while I was zigzagging between them at top speed, trying not to pee my pants.

I ran in the door, and standing in the lobby, was one of my bosses. He gave me a bizarre look as I flew past him yelling, "BATHROOM!"

I accepted an afternoon route one day that I thought would be a piece of cake. It was in my town; I knew the roads.

When I got to the bus, things got even better. It was a regular bus-tires out front-and there were no "turn arounds" on the route sheet.

I had a fine day, joking with the kids and not getting lost. Easy money; this bus thing wasn't so bad, after all. Or so I thought.

I got home and made myself a snack. A while later, the phone rang and the caller ID said it was the bus depot.

"They must want me to drive tomorrow," I thought, picking up the phone.

"Hi Dawn. Did you drive number 45 today?" the dispatcher asked.

"Yes," I happily answered.

"Did you realize when you parked it, you hit the pickup truck behind you?"

"Whaaaaa?" I thought I did so well, I didn't bother to check my parking job.

"Yeah; you pulled too far back and the underside of your bus tore up the hood of another driver's pickup truck.

I was flabbergasted. Even when I thought I did everything right, I stilled fucked-up. Fuck you Danny! Now my damn car insurance was gonna go up.

The way the parking lot was set up, one row of spaces lined the top of a small hill that had an almost vertical incline. The row behind it, was flush to the bottom of the hill. Had the lot been like a store parking lot, I would've been fine, but, because I was higher than the row behind me, I ran right over the fuckin' pickup and didn't even feel it.

I had to go to remedial school with all the other drivers who didn't know how to drive. The only saving grace was that I got paid for sitting in a classroom again.

Winter was a bad time to drive a bus where I lived. We get a lot of snow, which I never drive my car in. But, we needed the money, so I kept on driving.

I accepted a special needs route one day. I was disappointed when I found out it was a long, regular sized bus instead of a short one, but at least I had a nice, little old lady attendant to help me find my way. They were calling for snow that night, but for now, the roads were dry.

I checked the route sheet and saw that the drop-offs were way out in the boondocks, but, my lady would help me and it was extra hours on my paycheck.

We were dropping off the last kid when the first snowflakes fell. I knew we were pretty far from home, and just hoped we got back soon enough for me to get my car home safely.

Well, my car was the least of my concerns about fifteen minutes later. We must have been driving into the storm, because all of the sudden, it was pouring down snow and the road was covered. I slowed way down and gripped the wheel.

"Hold on," I yelled to my attendant. After I heard no response, my eyes left the treacherous road for a second to make sure the old thing hadn't died on me. The poor woman was in the back of the bus, white-knuckling the seat in front of her.

I was taking it easy for a while, then got cocky. Soon after I sped up just a little bit, the back of the bus swung to the right; I was sliding! I almost lost control of fifteen tons of metal in the middle of a snow storm.

"Drop the chains! Drop the chains!" the old woman was screaming frantically. I guess my driving was scaring her.

These newer buses had chains attached to them that would drop under the tires so you didn't have to stop, get out, and install them by hand. Pretty nifty invention; if I could only remember where the damn switch was to drop them.

I was searching the far reaches of my mind. We learned about the chains in class for about five minutes, months ago, and I didn't remember anyone ever actually showing me where the switch was.

With the cloud cover and the lateness of the day, I had to turn my overhead light on to see all the switches. I was trying to watch the road, read the dash and ignore the old lady that was still demanding that I drop the fuckin' chains!

I finally found the switch on the driver's door, hiding under a plastic cover that, thank God, said "chains". I flipped that bitch and heard them drop. They worked fabulous! No more sliding for me.

I came to a main road that must have been treated, because it hardly had any snow on it. I didn't know what to do. Should I pull the chains back up? But what if I slid again? I had never driven a fuckin' bus in the snow before; barely even in the rain; I was a fair-weather driver.

Well, when the sound of the chains clacking against the pavement made me think they were gonna pop the tires, I pulled them up.

Then we started sliding again. Before the old bitch could yell at me once more, I dropped the chains and just left them down the rest of way home. The old girl looked pretty shook up back there, and I didn't know how much more of this toboggan ride her heart could take.

I avoided driving on snowy days for the rest of my school bus driving career.

One fine spring day, I accepted a route. I shouldn't have. It was another route where the regular driver kept her bus at home. I should've know better.

When I went to pick up my spare bus, the man giving me the key started laughing again. You guessed it; when I found my bus, it was the fuckin' transit prison bus, with the fuckin' roundy mirrors-AGAIN!

I looked at the route sheet and at least knew the neighborhood for the elementary school kids. The older kid's route wasn't familiar, but they would help me.

I dropped off the last kid with hardly a curb hit, and started following the route sheet home. I was in the middle of a hundred-acre farm before I realized I was following the directions to the regular driver's house; not back to the bus depot. Shit!

There were fences everywhere, I was on a skinny dirt road, and I had to turn this bitch around with distorted mirrors. I couldn't believe this was happening!

I kept driving until I saw a narrow little driveway leading to a barn. I did a twenty-point turn around; slowly so I didn't hit a fuckin' fence, and finally got the damn bus turned around.

I drove out of the farm and pulled over. Now, I had to figure out how to read the directions backwards until I came to something familiar. I was so fuckin' lost.

After a while, and a few wrong turns, I found a main road that I knew would take my ass home. I was relieved and feeling pretty good; until I got to the parking lot. I drove in and the goddamn thing was full. The only open place in the whole lot, was the original spot I found this piece of shit parked in before.

I almost threw up! I was gonna have to maneuver this bastard bus into a space that was surrounded on all sides-and it had to be backed in-using the fucked-up mirrors!

I sat there looking at that spot. There was a storage shed behind it, a long bus on one side, a short bus on the other side and the worse part; the very explosive gas pumps were in front of it.

It wasn't like I had room to put the bus in position so I could back straight in, like the majority of the other parking spaces. Hell no! I had to do a backward turn with the roundy mirrors confusing my view of everything! I was royally fucked!

After several tries, and only getting the bitch halfway in the hole, I said "Fuck It! I need help."

I threw the gearshift in park and jumped out. I headed to the building to look for a boss, or at least another driver to park the bus for me. I went inside and it was a goddamn ghost town. I started searching the rooms and the only person in the whole shittin' ass place, was the custodian. Oh. My. God! I couldn't just leave the fucker hanging out of the parking space; I'd get in so much trouble.

I walked back outside and walked around the bus, trying desperately to figure out how the hell I was gonna park it. The mirrors were no help at all-I was gonna have to use the windows. I tried a few more times, then thought I had it. I slowly backed the bus in.

"Whew!" I let out the breath I hadn't realized I had been holding.

I checked the clock and filled out my timecard; at least I got a couple extra hours for all my stress. I gathered my stuff and jumped out to check my parking job. Standing in front of the bus, I was happy to see space on both sides. I needed to check the back to see how close I was to the shed. Cool! I didn't hit the fuckin' shed, not even a tap.

I was almost skipping around the other side, back to the front, because I was so happy this day was done. Then I came to a screeching halt.

At some point, trying to park that mother fuckin' bus, I had gotten too close to the bus next to me. There was a very long, very deep scratch, halfway down the side of the bus. Fuck. How did that happen? Maybe it was already there, I thought with hope; it was a very old bus.

Then I looked at where the scratch was compared to the bus next door. The other bus's side mirror, parallel to the scratch, was all fucked up. I must have hit the mirror, then dragged it along the side of my bus. I not only wrecked one bus; I wreaked two.

I never drove a fuckin' bus again!

MOVIE MAGIC

I'm a very nice person, but Danny knew how to push my buttons-sometimes to the point where I would disappear and an evil bitch would emerge.

On one such occasion, I happened to have the flu. I was so sick; I could barely get out of bed to go to the bathroom. Danny was actually working and I just had to drive him to the bus stop two miles away.

It was Sunday night and I told him I was just too sick and he would have to either walk or ride his bike to the bus stop-he said okay, no problem.

On Monday morning he woke me up to tell me that he overslept and missed the last bus-I would have to drive him the hour to work. I was furious! I did not want to drive for two hours in my condition but the fucker had to go to work or he would get fired. He volunteered to call in sick, of course, but I said no. I got out of my deathbed and got dressed.

I was driving down the road when I heard soft snoring. I glanced over to the passenger seat to find my husband sound asleep. Oh my God! I was damned if this fucker was gonna sleep all the way to D.C. while I drove for him trying not to puke.

The sharp, left-hand turn to get on the highway was coming up and a scene from a movie flashed in my mind. I was so mad; it didn't occur to me that I could've rolled the car if I recreated that scene.

Instead of slowing down to a safe turning speed, I gently hit the brake, waited until the last second, and turned the wheel as hard as I could.

His hungover, sleeping head slammed against the window. His eyes popped open, and he about jumped out of skin.

"Ow! What the fuck?" he yelled.

"Dodged a dog," I said.

DRUNK AND BLIND

One of the few pleasures I have left in life is watching TV. Even though it's not free anymore, my trips to the movie theater, or anywhere else fun, are few and far between.

I have certain programs that I love to watch, each night of the week. After a long, hard day of either working, cleaning or driving his ass around, I just want to crash in my chair, eat a snack and visit with my TV friends.

I came home from work one Saturday, and Danny told me I needed to call the cable company and get them to reset the box.

"Did you hit a wrong button on the remote again?" I asked. He was forever fuckin' up the TV because he just couldn't grasp the concept of how a remote worked.

"No, I was cutting the grass and accidentally ran over the cable to the dish."

"What?!" I exclaimed.

"Don't worry, I fixed it; but, the TV screen said we had to call for assistance."

"That's just fuckin' great," I said, pulling out my phone.

"I didn't do it on purpose! I didn't see it!" he slurred.

He didn't see it because he was drunk, putt puttin' his damn lawnmower around the backyard that had just been cut two days before, when he should've been doing something useful on the honey-do list I had left for him.

The tech tried to fix the TV remotely, but couldn't. Apparently he hadn't fixed the cable as good as he thought he did, because she told me we needed them to come out and install a new one.

She checked the schedule for the next time they would be in our area. She said that would be Tuesday. Fuckin' ass Tuesday! I'd have to go without TV for three goddamn days because he was a fuckin' idiot. I was livid.

INDIAN DANCE

Since he was out of work yet again, all he was doing was drinking all day; beer, no water or soda. He wouldn't eat anything until around 10:00 at night so as not to ruin his buzz, so his legs cramped all night cause he was so dehydrated.

No sooner would we all fall asleep, then he would wake up and start jumping around like an Indian doin' a fuckin' rain dance, his wails of pain echoing through the quiet house. Then we would all be awake.

Sometimes the cramps would last a few minutes, but sometimes they would last for hours. He would cry real tears and scream and moan. And we would have to endure that shit.

I begged him to drink a fuckin' glass of water for every beer he drank so this crap wouldn't happen, but he wouldn't. So he suffered. Night after night after night. I had no pity for his pain; it was his own damn fault.

TOILET

If he wasn't up in the middle of the night screaming like a banshee with the cramps, he was up, sitting on the toilet, smoking my damn cigarettes. More times than not, he would pass out while doing it.

I'd find him in the morning; dumbass sitting there naked, head and shoulders all hunched over. Sometimes the cigarette butt would still be pinched between his fingers; dead ashes on the floor. The other times the butt would have fallen from his hand while it was still lit. He ruined more throw rugs that way; I don't know how the house didn't go up in flames. I got tired of replacing rugs, so now there's yellow burn marks on the tile.

I honestly don't know how he didn't fall forward and bust his fuckin' head wide open.

HAPPY BIRTHDAY HAYLEY

I managed to come up with the money to give Hayley a birthday party.

Since I had planned it, decorated for it, and did everything else for it, Danny decided he wanted to carry the cake, blazing with candles, into the living room and set it before Hayley.

He had been drinking (it was a party after all) and I didn't want him to have that much responsibility. But he insisted. I didn't want to start a fight in a room full of people, so I let him do it.

I went out to stand next to my daughter and her friends that were gathered around the coffee table. When I saw him coming, I started singing "Happy Birthday."

He was balancing the cake pretty well while he was walking; I was impressed. But then he went to set it down in front of her.

I bought the huge, half sheet cake at the grocery store. The actual cake was on a piece of strong cardboard. The cake on the cardboard was in the plastic container. When Danny lifted the cake to bring it in, he brought it in on the bottom part of the container, the plastic part.

Danny bent over to set the cake down on the table and tilted it just a little bit. The cardboard started sliding off the plastic, headed straight for Hayley's lap. She saw it coming and jumped up before the candles could set her clothes on fire.

DOIN' THE LAUNDRY

One night, I was in my office working. I had just put a load of laundry in the dryer. A short time later, the dryer started making a very loud thumping noise. I hesitantly asked Danny if he could fix it; he was three quarters lit by that time. But, I was willing to let him try; the kids needed the clothes for the next morning.

About an hour later, he came into the office and told me he did the best he could, but we wouldn't be able to get into the basement because he had to move the dryer over the trap door in the floor.

"What?" I asked, puzzled.

"Come look," he said. "It's working fine, but you have to be careful with it."

"Oh, God," I said, getting up to go see what he did.

I walked into the laundry room and found the damn, running dryer tipped halfway over, the side of it leaning on top of one of my cardboard boxes full of junk.

"I fixed it!" he rejoiced.

"Oh my God!" I said, "That's not safe, what the hell were you thinking?"

Hayley had followed me into the laundry room, saw the fucked-up thing he did and started taking pictures on her phone. I think she posted them on the internet.

The next day, I went to work at an estate sale. A friend's kid was gonna bring over their extra dryer, and all I asked of unemployed Danny was for him to install it and finish all the laundry.

After a long, hard day, I walked through the door to find Danny laying on the couch, drinking his beer.

"Did you get the dryer installed?" I asked, hopeful.

"Not yet, but I did the laundry," he answered.

"How'd you do it without a dryer?"

"I made a clothes line," he said; like duh.

"What do you mean, you MADE a clothesline? We already have a clothesline."

"Come on, I'll show you," he said, excited to show me his invention.

After the way he "fixed" the old dryer, I was almost afraid to look. I followed him to the back door and looked out. The fuckin' idiot had made a clothesline, all right. He had rope tied from the porch to a tree, to the trampoline, to the shed, to another tree, back to the trampoline, to the swing set, and to the playhouse.

There were clothes all over my damn backyard, except on the real clothesline, which was empty as could be. He even had clothes laying on top of the new dryer he was supposed to install!

I just stood there, gapping at the spectacle. It looked like a goddam spider web made of clothes. I glanced next door, and there was my cute neighbor up on his deck, gapping at it too. Then in horror, I realized he was watching my big girl panties billow in the wind.

OVERFLOW

Even though his drinking and lack of goin' to work was financially devastating me and I just wanted him gone, there was one day I was happy he was there.

I was working on my computer when one of Hayley's friends used the bathroom adjacent to my office. She was in there for quite a while and the orchestra of wet, plopping sounds let me know the poor thing had diarrhea.

A few seconds after the toilet flushed, the door flew open and she said it was overflowing. I could see the toilet from my desk chair. I was horrified to see nasty, brown water with gobs of poop and toilet paper in it, spewing over the sides of the toilet.

I jumped up, ran in there, bent around the back and turned off the water; but the shit kept coming!

"Danny!" I screamed.

"What?" from the living room.

"Hurry; I can't stop the water!"

"I'm comin', I'm comin," he sang. I was sure he was moseying; he always moseyed everywhere without a fuckin' care in the world.

"I turned the water off, but it won't stop! Hurry!" I yelled with frustration.

By the time he got to the bathroom, the bathtub and the sink were filling with shit water and it was flowing out the door saturating my office rug. The stink was unbearable!

It took a few moments for him to realize what was happening.

"The sewer line's backed up. Quick, get me a pot!" he said, grabbing my clean towels off the shelf and using them to soak up the crap.

I ran and got the biggest pot we had and hurried back. Nastiness was still gushing from all the fixtures and my now shit-soaked towels were floating around in the bathtub. He had opened the window next to the bathroom door as wide as it would go and knocked the screen out.

He started panning the water, shit and toilet paper out the window. I had to leave the room; I couldn't breathe. I opened the office windows to let the wretched stink out and grabbed my laptop and phone. We needed a plumber; now.

I left messages at every plumbing service I could find. On a late Saturday afternoon, no one was open.

I guessed when the sewer line was empty, it would stop. I really hoped it was only our shit that flooded my house and not the whole fuckin' town's.

Danny came walking into the living room, looking beat, and the bottom of his jeans were soaked. He wasn't smellin' so good either.

"Okay, it stopped." he said.

"I talked to a plumber but he can't come till morning; and its gonna cost us," I informed him.

"How much?" he asked.

"Don't know, but it's off hours, so there's an extra charge."

He said okay cause he thought I could just go out back and shake the fuckin' money tree to pay for it.

The next morning, the plumber showed up. He stuck his snake down the hole in my floor and told me there was blockage.

"Well, no shit," I thought.

Then he told me he would have to stick a very expensive telescope down the hole to find out what it was; and it was gonna cost $1500.00 just to tell me what was there. I almost had a fuckin' heart attack, but what else could I do? The shower in the upstairs bath had broken a long time ago and we needed two toilets. I had no choice but to charge up our credit card some more.

I sat there and watched the guy hook up his laptop to the huge machine he had dragged through my house. He pushed more and more coil through the hole and finally it stopped.

"Look at this," he said, pointing to his computer screen.

It was like looking at a sonogram of a two-month old fetus; I didn't know what the hell I was seeing. I looked at him with a puzzled expression.

"It's a root ball," he said.

"What the hell's a root ball?" I asked.

"The roots from that big tree out front have broken through the pipe and tangled themselves up. Anything solid can't get through," he patiently explained, dollar signs shining in his eyes.

"How do we fix it?" I was already into this fiasco for $1500.

"You need to dig up the yard and replace the pipe. It's about twenty feet from the toilet to the root ball."

"Oh my God," I said, my mind racing to find a way to pay for this without having to mortgage the house.

"Would it be a lot cheaper if my husband did the digging and you just put the pipe in?" I asked hopefully.

He said yes and we headed outside so he could mark the ground where the pipe was. I waited while he grabbed what looked like a fancy ass metal detector from his truck. I lead the way around the house to the bathroom window and stopped cold in my tracks; my face burning red.

In Danny's haste to throw all the dirty water out the window, he didn't pay attention and threw everything that was on the floor out the window.

There, under the window that you could clearly see from the busy road (not to mention the church parking lot catty corner from my house), decorating my line of shrubs like Christmas ornaments, was a week's worth of my teenage daughter's thongs and bras, tinged brown by the fuckin' shit water.

RAW DOUGH DOWN BELOW

Aside from not having any sense, Danny always had something wrong with him physically. I didn't know if he was a fuckin' hypochondriac or if his body was just shutting down from all the years of abuse. But, it was always something; ailment after ailment.

I'd wake up to fresh blood on the sheets from his spontaneous bleeding. I'd awake in the night from his painful cries and see his shadow hopping around the room while he tried to get rid of his constant leg cramps. I'd be cruising him down the road and he'd start throwing up in his mouth because he was so hungover and my driving was making him sick. It never ended; I had become immune to it.

One Sunday morning, he came downstairs with a mortified look on his face and said, "We got problems."

"What now?" I asked, just knowing that fuckin' little shit cloud of his must have burst again.

"There's something wrong with my dick."

"Oh," I thought, relieved. "This wasn't OUR problem; it was HIS problem."

"What's wrong with it?" I casually asked.

"It's all swollen up," he said, unbuckling his pants.

He dropped his drawers, and I bit my tongue so hard it bled. Laughter was boiling up in me so fast and furious, it took everything I had to contain it. I had never seen anything like it! It was all fat and white and the head was tucked in like a turtle hiding from a predator.

I blurted out, "The little fella looks like a raw biscuit!" Cause it did.

If looks could kill, I'd be dead. Fire was shooting out his eyes!

"I'm sorry," I said with a giggle.

"What's wrong with it?" he whined, scared concern replacing the flames in his eyes.

I didn't know; I don't have a dick. So I googled it.

I had heard of inverted nipples before, so I typed in "inverted penis."

Nope. It didn't look like any of those pictures. So I typed in every other kind of penis I could think of, but nothing matched. I thought about seducing him to see if it would pop back out, but that made me throw up in my mouth.

Two Elderly Women And A Black Man

We could only afford to take the kids to Disney World every four years after I had accumulated enough Disney Dollars on my credit card to pay for park tickets. We had been conned into buying a fuckin' timeshare that first trip on the Auto Train, so we didn't have to pay for a hotel.

I had planned to drive down there (the whole way myself-still no license for dumbass) so pretty much, all we would have to pay for was gas and food. Then I informed him he couldn't drink in the car cause we would have pull over every damn hour so he could pee. This made him mad and he insisted we fly. I fought him, but he won. He promised he would work for the next four Saturdays to pay for the tickets-yeah, right.

On Monday we went to Hollywood Studios. We were having a great time until I figured how much he was spending on those beers he was buyin' every five minutes. I cut him off and the bitchin' started. He wanted to go back to the room and keep drinking (it was his vacation too, goddammit!) but I put my foot down.

The next day was "Magic Kingdom" day. As we were getting ready, a terrible thought popped into Danny's head.

"Is that the park where they don't serve beer?" he asked.

"Why yes; yes, I believe it is." I had forgotten about that; but it made me happy.

"You all go ahead, I'll just stay here," he said.

"No," I said sternly, "This is a FAMILY vacation and your ticket is already paid for; you can go one day without drinking. Just pretend it's a work day."

He saw the "that's final" look on my face and relented; but his balloon was popped.

The day before, we had taken the bus to the other park, and they dropped us off at the door. There were a lot of stops along the way though, so we decided to just drive and pay for parking. Bad decision; we should've took the bus.

We parked in a lot out in bum-fuck Egypt, hiked a while and waited for the tram to take us to the end of the parking lot. Then we hiked to the monorail to take us to the park, waited in line to go through security, then waited in line to go through the gate.

It was supposed to be dead this second week of December but the park was packed. Apparently, they were having Cheerleading Nationals or something, and there were kids everywhere!

We knew with the long lines, we were gonna have to pick and choose what rides we were gonna have time for. I let the kids circle the ones they wanted on the map, and our magical adventure began. All Danny wanted was a beer to nurse his hangover.

It got to be around lunchtime. Danny was in a foul mood and putting a damper on our day. This was the kid's favorite park and he was ruining it. Then he had a brilliant idea.

"Let's go back to the room and eat," he suggested. I knew he just wanted a fuckin' beer.

"I'm not going back through all that rigmarole," I said, "it'll take too long."

We found a restaurant that wasn't too expensive and bought lunch. He bitched through the whole meal, whining that he wanted to go back to the room and didn't see why I couldn't take him.

I finally couldn't take his shit anymore, and said, fine, I would take him back, but I wasn't about to make the girls leave the park. Annie was sixteen and had her cellphone, so I told her to take care of her sister while I took the asshole back to the room.

We were in the middle of the park, so we first had to make our way through a million people to get to the gate, then go through all the hiking and riding again to get back to the car. Then I had to drive him back to the resort and turn around and drive some more!

The parking lot was full by the time I got back, so I had to park even farther away. Then I hiked and rode back to the entrance again. More than two hours had passed since I had left and I was fuckin' exhausted. My legs were starting to hurt from my arthritis or fibromyalgia or whatever the hell was wrong with them, so I took some aspirin to get me through the rest of the day.

It took me a while to find the kids, but when I did, we had a fun, peaceful time.

We stayed until the park closed and on the way back, I saw a Krispy Kreme factory and the "Hot Donuts" light was on. The girls had never experienced the pure heaven of a hot Krispy Kreme melting in their mouth, so I pulled over. Most of the box of a dozen was gone by the time we got back and found Danny on the couch; drunk again.

The next day was Animal Kingdom day-where they did serve beer-so Danny went with us. Most of the day was fun, until I cut off his beer supply again. By the time we left, he was so grouchy I wanted one of the fuckin' lions to eat him.

All he wanted was to get back to the room, where his precious beer was waiting in the fridge. All me and the girls wanted was more Krispy Kreme doughnuts. He almost shit when I started driving the opposite way of the resort. He started bitchin'; then bitched some more. We didn't care; you couldn't get hot Krispy Kremes where we lived.

Annie was in rare comedic form that night, and with a spot-on British accent, she talked the whole way to the doughnut shop and the whole way to the resort. She was hilarious, and Hayley and I just laughed and laughed.

Danny was so mad his head looked like it was gonna pop off.

By the time we got to the elevator in the resort, he was furious. Me and the girls got in. He waited outside as the door slid shut, a "fuck you" expression plastered on his face.

On our floor, we stood at the bank of elevators waiting for his to arrive. When the light lit up, we got as close to the doors as we possibly could, and when they slid open, with a big smile on her face, Annie, in her British accent, said, "Ello D". Fire shot out his eyes as he stormed past us.

When we got back to the room, I informed him that we would have to forgo Epcot the next day and finish the Magic Kingdom. Since he made me leave the day before, and the girls didn't want to go on any rides without me, there was more magic to be had. I asked if he would be joining us.

"I ain't goin' nowhere with you fuckin' people," he said, slamming the door to the bedroom.

Well. Yaaayyy!

The next morning, the girls and I left for the park while he was still sleeping. I counted the beers in the fridge before we left; there were eight. I figured he would sleep until two and eight would be plenty. Eight beers was his turning point from jolly to jackass, so I knew when we returned, life was gonna be a bitch, but I wasn't prepared for what happened next.

When we got back to the room, Danny wasn't there. Hayley looked concerned, but I said not to worry; I was sure he was down at one of the pools. It was 9:30 by that time and I knew the pools closed at ten. All the beer was gone from the fridge, so I braced myself for the bastard to come through the door at any moment.

I was exhausted from walking all day and fell asleep on the couch.

A few minutes before ten, the room phone rang. Hayley answered it, woke me and told me it was the front desk. The only reason I could think of for their call was that they saw me smoking on the balcony and I was in trouble. If only it was that simple.

Bleary eyed, I said, "Hello?"

"Maim, your husband has been in an accident and has gone to the hospital."

"What?" I asked, my mind still foggy from sleep.

"He was very intoxicated and there was a lot of blood," the poor guy said.

"What happened to him?" I asked, coming fully awake.

"He said he was mugged by two elderly women and a black man. But witnesses say he slipped getting out of the hot tub and busted his head wide open."

Sweet Jesus! Two elderly women and a black man, my ass. Now the fucker was in the hospital and our health insurance hadn't kicked in yet from his most recent job. This cockamamie story made me question if he really did get mugged on the metro way back when, or if he just got in a fight and got his ass kicked.

The desk guy was still talking. He kept telling me over and over again how intoxicated Danny was, and how much blood he spilled. He said the EMT's had to force him into the ambulance. My head was spinning, but I think the guy said the cops came, too. I guess they would have had to, to take his police report about the "geriatric mugging."

When I didn't ask where they had taken my husband, because, frankly, I didn't care, he asked me if I wanted the address of the hospital. So, I said, "okay, give it to me." We were supposed to be on vacation and I didn't need to deal with this shit.

I wrote it down and hung up. I told the girls what had happened, and that we had to go to the ER. They couldn't believe it; I could. His fuckin' shit cloud had followed him to Florida.

We walked into the hospital lobby and the lady at the desk told us which cubicle he was in. We almost got to it, when a nurse came running over and told us we couldn't be back there and put us in a little tiny waiting room.

A few minutes later, we heard the unmistakable sounds of Danny yelling "Owwwww," at the top of his lungs. It was echoing through the thin walls for all to hear. We burst out laughing. I knew they were trying to put in an IV and couldn't find a good vein (all his veins were blown from drug use in his fucked-up youth). Served the asshole right.

A half hour passed, and no one came to get us. I peeked out into the hall and it was vacant and quiet. I told the girls we'd wait till midnight, and if nobody came, we were outta there.

Well, no one came, so we left. On the way out, the desk lady asked if I was ready to check him out; and pay, I assumed. I told her they were keeping him and we strolled out the door.

Early the next morning, I called him. He said he was ready to go. I wasn't about to deal with the bill, so I told him to go outside and I would pick him up at the door.

"No," he said, "somebody has to come in and check me out."

Fuckin' great; guess who was gonna have to deal with bill?

When I got to his room, a nurse was helping him to the bathroom and the doctor was there. I asked how he was, and the doc, who looked disgusted, told me he blew a .33 when they tested his alcohol level.

Gullible little me asked, "What's that mean?"

"It means, if it was me, I'd be dead," the nurse said.

When he staggered out of the bathroom, I realized the fucker was still drunk.

He must have pissed off the nurses, because they didn't clean him up very well; there was dried blood all over him.

As the doctor was examining him, he told me there were ten staples in the back of his head and he would have to be watched all day.

"But we're going to Universal today," I said.

"He has a head injury. Someone has to stay with him or we can't release him. We can admit him if you want, and put him under observation."

I didn't know how the hell we were gonna pay for the ER visit, much less a hospital stay, so I said I would watch him. He was still much too shaky to be released, so I had to sit there and wait for the fucker to sober up.

When we were alone, I asked, "What the hell happened to you?"

"I got mugged," he said, the spoonful of scrambled eggs shakily aiming for his mouth.

"Bullshit, Danny! You were wasted and fell down. How did you blow a .33 from only eight beers?"

"I went to the pool bar and had some ice teas."

Long fuckin' Island ice teas, loaded with liquor! He knew damn well he couldn't ply liquor on top of beer, or bad things would happen.

"If you busted the back of your head, why do you have a black eye?" I asked; his blood smeared face was also black and blue.

"The EMT hit me," he said.

"Why would he hit you?"

"Cause I wouldn't get in the ambulance; I was scared about the money."

I noticed the plastic bag with his belongings in it, so I looked inside. All that was in there, was his soaking wet swim trunks; no shirt, no shoes and no wallet.

"Where's your wallet?" I asked, concern growing.

"I told you I got mugged."

"You are so full of shit! You honestly don't know where your wallet is?"

"No, Dawn; I told you."

"Yeah, yeah, I know, you got mugged. Did you maybe leave it in the room?"

"No, cause I went to the bar."

"Well, now I'm gonna have cancel the fuckin' credit card." I wanted to leave him in that hospital forever.

They finally released him three hours after I had gotten there. On the way out, the nurse looked at me with pity in her eyes, and told me how sorry she was. I said not to worry; it's always like this. The pity deepened. I was really tired of people feeling sorry for me because he's a goddam idiot.

He was wearing paper scrubs, his face was multi-colored from the blood and bruises, and the hair on the back of his head was all matted with dried blood and there was a big, bald spot centered with a line of staples. He was a goddamn, fucked-up mess. And he still wasn't completely sober.

An orderly rolled him outside in a wheel chair, right past the front desk where I thought he would stop so I could pay. I kept my mouth shut and kept going.

A few minutes down the road, I heard snoring coming from beside me. I looked over, and Fucker was sound asleep; lit cigarette in his hand that was resting on his paper pants, the red hot cherry ready to drop off and set him on fire. What the hell was WRONG with him?!?

I wanted to lean over, open the door and push his ass out of the car.

I had a thought as we pulled into the resort parking lot. No, not walk him to the beautiful fountain and hold his head under water til he was dead. Most other women who have put up the shit I have would've done that, but not me. I thought, hopefully, someone had put his stuff in the lost and found.

I pulled up to the security building and left his half dead ass in the car with the windows rolled up. I told the officer who I was.

Thank God! She pulled his shirt and shoes out from under the counter, and tucked in the toe, was his wallet, intact.

To get to our room, I would have to walk Danny, in all his horrifying glory, through the busy lobby to the elevators. When I managed to get him out of the car, the staring began.

I had to practically carry his staggering ass through the crowded lobby; I was mortified. Little kids wearing mouse ears were ducking behind their parents when they saw the scary man coming towards them. I just tried not to make eye contact with anybody.

No one wanted to ride the elevator with us.

I got him to the bed, then went to tell the girls the bad news induced by Danny; we couldn't go anywhere cause daddy had once again, ruined our vacation. They were devastated. I was too.

I went out on the balcony to have a cigarette and call my friend. I told her what happened and she said, if it was her, she'd leave his fuckin' ass there and let the girls finish their vacation. So, that's just what I did.

By the time we made it to Universal Studios, it was almost one in the afternoon. The place was packed and we had to pay extra for speed passes so we could hit most of the rides.

I was silently hoping that head injury would kill him and release me from my misery. But it didn't.

I confiscated Danny' credit card before we got on the plane so he couldn't buy any alcohol. Because we couldn't afford good plane seats, all four of us were split up. I sat dumbass in the seat between two fat men so he'd be squished all the way home; I wanted him to suffer. Fucker shouldn't have ruined my vacation.

AFTERMATH

Even though Danny had told his job of our impending trip to Disney World when he was hired, they still fired his ass when we got back. They told him it was because he missed a week of work, but that was bullshit. Danny's fuckin' bad work ethic had struck again.

The Florida doctor had told us Danny needed to have the staples taken out of his head after ten days; it had already been eleven. I had forgot and Danny seemed content just to leave them in there.

We had no fuckin' health insurance, and no money for a self-pay doctor's visit. I thought about taking those little bastards out myself with my staple remover, but was scared he'd get infected and have to go to the hospital again.

So I took him to the vet's office where I worked and had my friend rip 'em outta his fuckin' head. Like he was a dog.

FEELING THE BURN

Danny found a new job and was doing well there. We almost made it to spring before his shit cloud started to rain.

He called me from work and told me to come get him.

"Did you get fired AGAIN?" I asked.

"No." He sounded shocked that I could even think such a thing. "I blew my shoulder out."

Dammit! More doctor bills and more time off work.

When I took him to our family doctor, she sent him to a specialist. He had really fucked up his shoulder; on purpose so he could stay home and drink? I wondered.

He ended up being off work for five weeks; five weeks that he didn't bring in any money. During his hiatus, he suggested we start rolling our own cigarettes to save money. God forbid he quit drinking.

So, I went on eBay and found a little cigarette rolling machine for twenty bucks and ordered it. When the machine came in, Danny and I went to the tobacco store to buy the filtered tubes and some tobacco. Rolling our own would be a pain in the ass, but it knocked about 85% off the price of a pack of cigarettes.

We set up our cigarette station and started rolling. They didn't taste as good, but I was getting my nicotine and my needs were being met. He didn't like them all, but I didn't give a shit. I told him if he wanted to give up his beer, he could buy all the Marlboro Reds he wanted. He decided he would get used to the taste.

And so, the year of "Feeling the Burn" began.

The cheap machine I bought was a piece of shit and it didn't pack the cigarettes right. They would either fall apart when we were smoking them or burn sideways. It was fuckin' weird, but since they were practically free, I kept rolling.

We thought the tobacco was too thick, so Danny started screening it like he used to do his weed. This helped a little; they didn't burn sideways anymore at least, but I think it killed the hamster.

Because of the cats, we had to keep little Smokey in a glass aquarium with a screen top; the screen Danny used to thin out the tobacco. The hamster would constantly climb on top of its wheel to try to escape.

After Danny would screen, he would just put it back on the cage without cleaning out the pieces of tobacco that were stuck in the holes. I think Smokey was eating it and poisoning herself. After a while of this, Hayley found her dead.

We're really lucky those homemade cigarettes didn't set the fuckin' house on fire because they did everything else.

The first time it happened, I was minding my own business, sitting in my chair, watching TV. I took a drag and the damn thing was dead. Thinking that it had just went out, I relit it.

I happened to glance down and my fuckin' seat was smolderin'. I was gonna have to be more careful, I thought. But sometimes, I just plum forgot.

I was driving down the road one day, smoking, and I started to hear a sizzling noise in my left ear.

"What the hell *is* that?" I thought to myself; right before I smelled burning hair. I looked at my cigarette; no cherry.

The wind from my cracked open window had blown the cherry onto my shoulder where my long hair was laying. I set my damn self on fire. I set so many fires in the car; you'd think I'd stop smoking in there.

One day, I had all the kids in the car. I was wearing leggings and Uggs boots. We were cruising down the highway, jamming to some tunes, when I felt a burning sensation on my foot. I looked at my cigarette and thought, "Oh, Shit!"

The fuckin' cherry had fallen off my cigarette right into my boot! There was nowhere to pull over, so I kicked my boot off, reached between my legs to grab it and handed it to Annie.

"What do I do with it?" she asked; eyes wide, holding my smoking, stinky boot.

"Roll down the window and dump out the cherry," I yelled before flames could start shooting.

She was freaking out, the kids in the back were laughing and I was praying the child wouldn't drop my $200 boot out the window.

Another time, I was on my way to the store when I set myself on fire. My hair escaped this time cause I had it pulled up. When I took a drag and nothing came out, I saw that the cherry was missing. I didn't see any smoke or smell anything, so I just thought it fell out the window when I flicked an ash.

A minute or two later, after I rolled the window back up, I smelled smoke; then saw it drift around the side of my head. I started patting frantically at the back of my neck, but the smoke kept coming. I was wearing a hoodie, so I pulled to the side of the road and ripped it off.

The damn cherry had blown off when I flicked the ash, but instead of going out the window, the wind caught it (just like that stink bug Danny ate) and it flew back in and landed inside my hood. I couldn't feel anything because the jacket was so thick.

Had my window still been open and blowing the smoke to the backseat where I wouldn't notice it, my damn head might have gone up in flames.

I set my gut on fire once, driving down the road. I carry most of my poundage around the middle, so when the cherry fell off as

I was taking a drag one day, I didn't notice when it settled on my protruding tummy. It burnt a hole in my shirt and started to blister my belly before I felt it and could put it out. Of course, I almost wrecked while doing so. I started slapping at the cherry and burning ashes were flying everywhere.

Sometimes, I didn't even feel it; I just noticed random, little, scorched holes in my clothes. My car seats are ruined. Both front seats are pock marked with singed holes; Danny set fires too. My desktop has burn marks and is forever covered with ashes where the cherry drops unnoticed while I'm on the computer.

I had my favorite blue, corduroy jacket sitting on the kitchen counter one time. Drunk ass Danny was rummaging through the cabinets overhead, and I guess he thought my jacket was an ashtray. After he settled on the couch with his peanut butter and jelly sandwich, I noticed the kitchen was smoky.

"Did you cook something?" I asked.

"No, just made me a sammich," he said as he chewed. I hated when he used that word.

"Well something's burning," I said, jumping up.

I ran into the hazy kitchen and saw my damn coat in flames. Freaked out by the fire that was ready to lick my cabinets, and coughing on smoke, I grabbed the blazin' bundle. Instead of throwing in the sink that was right there and extinguishing it with water, I hauled ass to the back door.

I flung that thing as far as could away from the house. It sailed across the yard like a flamin' arrow. I always sucked at softball so of course it fell in a pile of trash Danny had neglected to pick up. Now my fuckin' yard was scorched.

I had gone to pick Danny up from work, and like always, lit a cigarette for the drive home. My car door has a molded pocket on the inside, which I use as a trashcan. I always keep a lot of napkins in the car because I'm always sneezing and he's always throwing up. When I finish blowing my nose, I crumple up the napkin and drop it into the pocket. Since I rarely clean out my car, this pocket is always pretty full of paper.

We were pulling out of his parking lot, and I was talking away, telling him about my day before he could start bitchin' about his, when I saw the smoke. Apparently the cherry had dropped off once again and this time, dropped in my makeshift waste basket.

"Oh, shit," I said calmly, "the door's on fire."

"Well pull over!" Danny exclaimed.

I looked down, and when I didn't see any illumination, said, "It's okay, I got it."

I reached in and grabbed the wad of searing napkins and chucked 'em out the open window.

I watched it through my side mirror. Before it hit the ground, it burst into flames. When it completed its short trip to the asphalt, it looked like a cute little campfire there in the middle of the road. This made me laugh really hard.

I looked over at Danny. He didn't see the humor.

HOTEL HELL

When I couldn't take his drinking and lack of employment anymore, I threw his ass out. I hoped without me taking care of absolutely every damn thing he would get his shit together. He didn't.

I put him in the cheapest hotel I could find, far enough away so he couldn't walk home and gave him the only credit card in his name; it had about $3500 left on it. He didn't have a dime in his pocket, but could use the credit card for everything he needed. I told him he couldn't come back until he was sober and employed for while-I wasn't gonna be his mother anymore.

A few days later, I decided to check his purchases to see what he was up to. I logged into his credit card account and started looking. The night I dropped him off, he went straight to the gas station and bought a six pack (cause God knows the no-drivin' shit didn't need gas for anything). The hotel charge was there, enough for three days. I guess he thought I would miss him in three days-haha.

The next day, more beer and some fast food.

The day after that was a little concerning. Not only were there beer and food charges, it appeared drunk Danny had found the local bar-and by the amount of the charge, had a really good time. I thought that was just fuckin' fantastic. If he had moved on to mixed drinks, he would burn his way to his credit limit in no time.

I scrolled down the page to a new day. This was interesting- there was a charge for a new hotel; one that cost almost $50 more a night. What was this idiot thinking? While I knew he didn't know jack about finances, I couldn't imagine he was that dumb. I called the original hotel to find out if they had a pool. Danny loved to swim and if the first hotel didn't have a pool, maybe he found one that did.

Turns out, homeboy got thrown out of the first hotel. That night he found the bar, he stumbled back, got in fights with the other guests, broke things and spilled his blood everywhere.

After a couple of days of living in the fancy hotel, he called me and begged to come home. I said hell no, but agreed he couldn't keep living high on the horse. I drove east and picked him up. Then I drove west, past our town and even farther away from the house than before. I came to the first dumpy hotel I could find and made him check in. It was only $39 a night.

The town was more like a little city and there were hundreds of places for him to look for a job, and cheap bus service to get him there. I still had hope he would straighten up, be a man and we could live a normal life. I was an idiot.

A few nights later he called me crying. Apparently, I had stuck him in a Crack hotel where all the rooms were filled with druggies who lived there all the time. He said he got in a fight with two guys and they were coming back to kill him; I had to come get him NOW!

I told him there was no way I was walking into that; I didn't want to fuckin' die. I told him to call the cops if he thought his life was in danger. He said he did and they wouldn't come. I told him that was bullshit and he was making the whole thing up. So he put me on the phone with his "neighbor" who told me that yes, indeed, Danny was gonna get murdered if I didn't come save him. I still didn't go, but he lived anyway.

About a week later, he called and told me he was coming home and there was nothing I could do about it. So I changed the locks on the doors and told all the neighbors to call the police if they saw him trying to get in. I guess he couldn't find a ride, cause I never came home to finding him laying on my couch.

Two months had passed and I kept tracking the credit card. There were beer charges every day, sometimes two or three times a day. But there weren't any bus charges or any indication he had found a fuckin' job. Some days there weren't even any food charges. I decided to go there and take him grocery shopping so at least he would have some peanut butter and jelly to eat. I had thrown him out in August with only shorts and t-shirts, so I packed him up some warmer clothes.

I knocked on his door, hoping he wouldn't answer, that he was out job hunting. But no, I heard footsteps coming.

The door opened and I was taken aback. He was almost unrecognizable. He had drank so much, his liver wasn't functioning properly and he was so puffed up, he looked like his skin was gonna pop!

He left the door open and went to lay on the bed. I followed him in, sat in the chair and asked what he had been up to. He said, "pretty much what you see." Well, all I saw was him layin' there trying to drink himself to death.

I asked how the job hunt was going and he told me he applied at three places but nobody wanted him. Two months, hundreds of stores and restaurants, and the dumbass only applied at 3 places? What the hell was wrong with him? I told him that I had paid his credit card bill last month but couldn't afford to this month and it was coming due-he better walk over to McDonald's and make some fuckin' money. So then, we started arguing and I finally stood up and said let's go to the store to get you some food.

He stood up and held out his arms and for a second, I thought he was gonna give me hug. But instead, he spun me around, escorted me to the door and promptly threw me out saying he didn't need my fuckin' food. Well! I got in my car and went home.

*

A couple more weeks went by, the credit card was maxed out and he was no longer at the hotel. I had no idea where he was; I thought maybe he had made camp in a bush again. Or, maybe those guys came back and killed him. At this point, I didn't give a shit.

Then I got the call from a social worker at the hospital. When he ran out of credit, he had checked himself in. With no money for beer, he started detoxing and thought he was gonna die. She said they were gonna have to release him soon and all the homeless shelters were full and I needed to come get him.

Well, no, that wasn't gonna happen. The girls and I were happy as little larks without him. We painted the living room purple and hung a crystal chandelier. We were turning our home into a princess house and didn't want the nasty old troll to come back. Ever.

A couple nights later, it was cold and pouring down rain and my phone rang. It was Danny. He was freezing and had nowhere to go. He swore he was sober and his liver was shot and promised he would never drink again. Would I please, please let him come home?

I told him that wasn't the deal, to go find an all-night diner to sit in and find a job in the morning if he was sober. Well, he wailed and begged some more until I finally told him it was up to the girls. Annie told me to give him one week to find a job; if he didn't, he was back out the door.

Sober, But Still A Moron

I let him recuperate from his ordeal for a couple of days, then made him get on the bus to go look for a job. One of the conditions of his coming home was that he would be a self-sufficient grown-up. He would have to huff it to the bus stop on foot; I had better things to do than drive him.

That evening, when it was about time for the bus to bring him home, a police car sped by our house with its sirens and lights on, in the direction Danny would be coming from.

Hayley jokingly said, "They're probably going after daddy."

I laughed and said, "Probably." But when he didn't come home soon after that, I thought maybe they really were speeding down the road after him. I told Hayley we probably should go look for him.

Walking to the car, we saw him strolling down the street.

"You won't believe what just happened," he said when he got close enough. "The cops just pulled me over for walking."

His fuckin' black shit cloud was still hanging over his head.

He said that he was walking down the dark road where there was no sidewalk and a car was coming. Rather than get hit, he ran over to the side and jumped in the bushes. Apparently the driver saw him, thought he looked shady and called the cops.

They gave him a drunk test on the side of the road; for all my neighbors to see.

ER's, Doctors And The Fuckin' DMV

Danny found a job where one of his old bosses was now the manager; one of the very few old bosses that actually liked him. It was a cheap bus ride away and he could get there on his own. He was totally sober, making money and we were getting along-the house was peaceful. He didn't approve of the purple living room, but it wasn't his fuckin' house-he was just glad he had a roof without leaves growing out of it.

Two days after Danny started his new job, I came home from work to find him sitting on the couch looking very weird. It was a Saturday, so I knew he hadn't been fired.

"What's wrong?" I asked.

"I don't know. My heart's been beating out of my chest for about an hour and I can't slow it down."

I walked over and grabbed his wrist to check his pulse. It was definitely racing.

"Does your left arm hurt?" I thought he was having a heart attack.

"It's a little numb." Shit! I finally got him clean, sober and gainfully employed, and now the fucker was gonna drop dead on me.

"Get in the car; we're going to the ER," I said.

They took him in right away. His heart was beating at 165 beats per minute.

They gave him a drug that immediately dropped his heart rate, but it made his blood pressure go up.

They ran all the heart tests on him and discovered he had an arrhythmia. They wanted to observe him overnight, so I went home to the girls.

I guess when they were in the computer recording Danny's results, they found all his info from his last hospital stay and gave him more tests. He ended up staying in the hospital for four days and I had to call him in sick to work. I knew this normal life shit was too good to be true.

Danny came home from the hospital with thirteen different prescriptions; it took me a fuckin' hour to have them all filled at the pharmacy. There were meds for his heart and liver, and also two high powered antibiotics. Danny's blood had gotten infected while he was in the hospital (his black cloud struck again). And so began my unchosen career as an unpaid nurse.

I spent the next month running him all over Northern Virginia to doctor's appointments; and to and from the bus stop. He was missing at least one day of work a week. Opportunist that he is, even if the appointment was only gonna take an hour, dumbass took the whole day off.

I learned from the gastrologist that Danny's damaged liver was throwing off ammonia that would travel to his brain and cause hallucinations if he didn't get it out of his body. Well, that explained why he did stupid shit all the time. He had to take medicine to make him poop three times a day; that's how he got rid of the ammonia. We were going through toilet paper like there was no tomorrow.

A couple weeks after he left the hospital, I went to work and shortly after I got there, he called and said his heart was racing again; faster than before.

I went home straight away, and found him pale and breathing heavy. I felt his pulse and the bitch was racing faster than the last time. I told him to get in the car, we were going to the ER.

This time it was beating at 225 beats per minute. The doc gave him the drug and it lowered it. Danny also told the ER doctor that his stomach had been hurting really bad. They did an x-ray. Danny had gall stones. They let him leave after a couple of hours and gave him a bottle of heart pills, with directions to get more from his family doctor.

Shit was popping up all over this man and making my damn head spin.

Aside from driving him to all his doctor appointments, and making trips to the ER, I had to administer the thirteen medications, once, twice or three times a day. He just couldn't figure it out.

I was getting more and more frustrated by the day. I didn't sign up for this shit when I let him come home. I thought I was getting a man who had finally gotten rid of his demons and could take care of himself. Instead I got a sickie who went from a troubled teenager to a large baby.

It wasn't just his health problems that were dominating my life that month. The goddamn DMV was taking what little time I had left for myself, my jobs and my children. Long story short, after at least ten trips to the DMV, at least two hours a piece, 2 trips to court, several trips to ASAP and a shitload of money spent for this and that, all fucker got was a restricted Learner's Permit which didn't help me at all! Apparently, Danny had lost his driver's license before the computer age and they didn't believe he ever had one.

I was getting meaner by the day. I was thoroughly exhausted. I wasn't making any money because I was spending all my time taking care of him.

I was not happy with Danny at all; I was ready to kill him. I know that sounds terrible; sickness and health, for better or for worse and all that crap. But the way I saw it, everything he was going through was of his own making. All of his health problems could be traced back to his lifestyle. All of his driving problems could be traced back to his lifestyle.

The Monday after New Year's, Danny went to work. He was feeling much better and was ready to kick ass and make money; music to my ears. Then the black cloud had another blow-out.

He called me around mid-morning.

"Bad news," he said, "they let me go for missing too much work. Come and get me."

I can't count how many times I got that same goddam phone call over the years beginning with "Bad news". The same old shit was still happening, but instead of being hung over, he was sick.

He wanted me to drive for an hour to come get him. I told him to hop a bus and find another job.

He didn't. He slept eighteen to twenty hours a day; the poor thing was depressed. I don't know if he thought I was growing a field of fuckin' money trees in the backyard or what, but he didn't seem to worry about how the bills were being paid.

Of course, all his non-productive sleeping was pissing me off. During his waking hours, all we did was fight and he would hog my damn TV. He'd watch old movies, which would drive me crazy. I would be trying to work and the monotone dialogue and crappy music would practically put me to sleep. I was about ready to poison his food.

He also bitched that the house was too cold. Well, our fuckin' oil bill was almost $400 a month on the budget plan, so I bought a few space heaters and kept the house heater turned off. It was chilly, but the kids weren't complaining; we just wore sweat shirts.

All Danny did was complain. He would watch TV with his coat, hat and gloves on. He would sleep in his boots. I thought he was just being a big, fat baby, so I told him to quit bitchin' and throw another blanket on. He was ridiculous; you couldn't see his breath.

His Shit Cloud Was Snowing Now

The blizzard hit on January 22, 2016. Danny had been asleep for almost a month. The kids were off school for a week. I didn't know it when the first snowflake hit the ground, but we were headed for the week from hell.

The day after it stopped snowing, sleeping beauty woke up and decided he was gonna dig the car out; I guess he didn't want me to miss work. I told him to take it slow, he might have a heart attack. At that point in our volatile relationship, I didn't really care if he had a heart attack; I just didn't want to have to deal with the aftermath.

He came in and asked me to take him to the store; he needed soda.

"Is the car all cleaned off?" I asked.

"Everything but the top," he said.

"Danny. I can't drive with that much snow on the fuckin' roof. Didn't you see the news? Snow's been flying off cars, hitting windshields and killing people."

"I wasn't gonna put that much snow back in the driveway. It can fall in the street where the plows will get it."

What a dumbass.

"I ain't doin' it," I told him, "drink water."

So he stomped back outside.

That night, I was sound asleep and dreaming.

"Dawn," I heard, and someone was pokin' me.

"What?"

"My heart's racing again; I need to go to the hospital," Danny breathed.

"What time is it?" I asked, bewildered. One minute, I was dead asleep, the next, he's towering over me, wanting me to go outside in the snow.

"3:30," he said, "my heart's been racing for half an hour."

He grabbed my hand and slapped it on his chest to feel the beat; I almost fell out the fuckin' bed."

Oh my God, I couldn't believe this was happening. I was exhausted. The last thing I wanted to do was go to the emergency room, listen to him scream while they tried to find a good vein, then sit there for two hours while they observed him.

"Don't you have any of those heart pills left?" I moaned.

"I finished those a long time ago. You were supposed to," he began.

"You were supposed to. You were supposed to. YOU were supposed to call the fuckin' doctor," I yelled, cutting him off. "Why is it ALWAYS up to me to do EVERYTHING concerning you? I'm not your mother!"

"Forget it then. I'll just call an ambulance."

"You can't. We can't afford it," I said, and huffed and puffed out of the bed. I grabbed my clothes and went to the bathroom. I sat there smoking a cigarette; fuming.

He was sitting on the steps outside my door, taking deep breaths. My mind was desperately searching for an excuse not to go.

"There's black ice on the road; I could wreck," I offered between drags.

He was still breathing heavy, his hand over his heart.

Then I became fully awake and remembered that in his drinking days, he was always complaining about his heart racing. He thought he was having anxiety attacks. He never went to the hospital then and he didn't fuckin' die. I put this out there for him to ponder. When he didn't respond, I guessed I was going to the goddamn hospital.

When I was done with my cigarette, I put my clothes on. I walked up behind him and he grabbed my hand again, and slapped it over his heart.

"I think its slowing down. We'll wait a while. I don't want to go any more than you do," he said.

Well, the beat didn't feel any slower, but I wasn't one to look a gift horse in the mouth! I said "Okay" and went back to bed.

The next morning, Monday, I peeked in on him. I stood there at Hayley's bedroom door (where he had been sleeping since he came home), trying to see if he was breathing. I didn't have my glasses on, but thought I saw the blanket moving. Good. He wasn't dead. My house was old and the hall was narrow; there was no way the EMT's could get a stretcher down it to retrieve his body.

On Wednesday morning I went to work, leaving the kids at home with Danny. I figured he'd just sleep all day like he had been, and wouldn't be any trouble for them.

When I got home, the girls were playing video games.

"Has he gotten up all?" I asked.

"Oh, yeah," Annie said, giving me a disgusted look.

"What happened?" I asked, dreading her answer.

"I was in my room, and he shuffled in with his cup. He asked if I would go downstairs and get him some soda. I said I would. When I took it in to him, he said I forgot the ice. So I went back downstairs to get the ice. When I got back, he was throwing up in the cup. I wasn't gonna get him more soda."

Jesus, Mary and Joseph! Could he not even make it ten fuckin' feet to the bathroom to puke?

Throughout the rest of the day, we could hear him up there violently throwing up his guts. We stayed downstairs.

About 8:30 that night, he emerged from the bedroom. He looked like shit! Puffy face, two black eyes from bustin' his blood vessles, fuckin' hair sticking every which way.

"What's wrong with you?" I asked, trying to sound concerned, but I wasn't.

"I've been throwin' up all day. There was blood in it. My stomach hurts bad."

Here we go again.

"You know; you have an appointment with the liver doctor next Thursday. You can call tomorrow and see if they can get you in any earlier," I suggested.

But, of course, he didn't call. That would require he actually get out of the bed and do something.

Friday morning, I woke up and walked out of my room to find Danny standing in Hayley's doorway. His head was hung low and he had a long piece of board tucked under his armpit like a crutch. I had no idea where the wood came from; I had never seen it before.

"You're not gonna believe what happened," he said, shaking his head. "I broke my leg."

Un-FUCKING-believable! The lengths this man would go to get out of going to work. Just the night before, I told him if he didn't get some kind of a job, we were gonna be homeless and I didn't want to be a fuckin' hobo.

I didn't see any bones sticking out, so I told him he probably just sprained it. He said he needed to go to the hospital. What was it with him and the damn hospital? Nobody likes to go to the fuckin' hospital.

I said no; there wasn't anything they could do for a sprain. I told him to elevate his leg. Then, to seem interested, I asked him how it happened. He was already plucking my nerves and I had only just rolled out of the goddamn bed!

"I tripped on the mattress that was on the floor. I've been crying all night; I don't know how you didn't hear me." I probably did, but my sleeping head didn't care.

Mattress on the floor? you might be asking. Beside collecting heavy man junk that I can't easily dispose of, Danny liked to bring home every goddam mattress that I couldn't sell at an estate sale, searching for the one that would give him the perfect night's sleep. He piled them high on everyone's bed. I needed a set of library steps to get in mine.

Hayley had had a friend over and they decided to make a slide out one of her mattresses and it ended up on the floor, and apparently Danny took a tumble on it.

I just shook my head and walked to the bathroom. As I was sitting there smoking a cigarette, I could hear him moaning and groaning; in pain, I guess.

In my mind, I was asking God, "WHY? WHY? What was next?"

Then I heard his fuckin' cup of ice water hit the floor; the water splashing against the wall; him saying "Shit."

"What was that?" I pleasantly asked, already knowing.

"My glass of water," he whined. "It took me an hour to get it."

It took everything I had not to bust out laughing.

"Do you know where the crutches are?" he moaned.

"I think they're in the basement."

"Oh, no," he said grimly. He knew I wasn't gonna drag my big ass down to the cellar.

"They're in the back room," Hayley's little voice called from my bed.

"I'll look," I sighed, going down the stairs.

I found them in the back room. I trudged halfway back up the stairs and stuck them through the railings to him. All I wanted at this point was my first cup of coffee and not to have to look at his sorry ass. It was just one fuckin' thing after another with him.

As I passed him the crutches, he held his empty cup out to me, and with pleading eyes, said, "Will you get me some more water?"

Oh my God!

He was sitting on the fallen mattress, not making any fuckin' attempt to move; I was on the stairs, not able to reach the cup. So, dammit, I carried myself up the rest of the stairs, down the hall and grabbed the cup out of his hand.

He watched me walk back down the hall, and almost to the bottom of the stairs before saying, "You could have just gotten the water from the faucet up here."

I hated him.

While I was making my precious coffee, I glanced out the window. Goddammit! It was snowing again. How in the hell was he gonna dig my damn car out with a broke-ass leg? I'm screwed.

Later that morning, I went to the vet's office to work. The snow didn't last long and I didn't need to dig my car out.

When I got there, I filled Peggy and Susie in on my fucked-up morning with Danny. I no sooner logged into Quickbooks when my cellphone rang.

"It's probably him," I said. But it was Annie. I had Hayley with me, but poor Annie was at the house with him.

"Mom," she said, sounding like she was gonna break at any moment, "Danny said he broke his leg and he wants me to take him to the emergency room. I told him I would call you and he said 'She ain't gonna take me.'" She could hear the loathing in his voice when he referred to me.

I put her on speaker phone so the girls could hear the continuing saga.

"He just sprained his knee, honey, there's nothing the emergency room can do for him. I'm trying to work."

"Well he has to go to the bathroom. I tried to help him up and couldn't."

"Honey, just give him an empty bottle."

"I did. He said he doesn't have to *pee*."

Me, Hayley and my co-workers all burst out laughing.

"Can you please come home; I don't know what to do," Annie pleaded.

"I should get him a fuckin' Life Alert," I growled.

"Mommy, please," Annie begged, "I don't know what to do!"

"Okay, honey. I'm coming," I said; frustrated because I had work to do.

When I hung up the phone, Susie said, "Peggy, can you get her something to wrap his knee?"

"I'll do better than that," Peggy said, heading for the door. "I'll get him a kitty litter pan to poop in."

We all thought that was a magnificent idea.

I was furious. There I was, trying to make whatever money I could to pay our fuckin' bills because that son-of-a-bitch hadn't brought in a single dime in thirty days, and now I had to go home and nursemaid him again.

I got home and went upstairs. I had no intention of being a sweet Florence Nightingale.

"What's wrong now?" I said, holding his poop pan and leg wrap.

"I'm in so much pain," he heavily breathed, "I need to go the emergency room."

"There's nothing they can do for you. Let me see your leg," I barked. I couldn't help it. I did not want to spend the rest of my day in the damn ER. I had had it with him!

"I heard my knee pop when I fell," he explained.

His knee wasn't swollen, bruised or anything; but I was gonna wrap it anyway.

He started to pull up the leg of his sweat pants, and I said, impatiently, "NO, take them off. I have to wrap your knee."

It took him five fuckin' minutes to pull his pants down. I got frustrated and decided to help. I was not gentle.

"Ow, Ow, Ow," he screamed, tears springing to his eyes, mouth wide open, naked gums gleaming at me.

"Where's your teeth?" I exclaimed, mortified.

"On the dresser," he cried, "Why ya bein' so mean to me?"

"I'm not. Straighten out your leg so I can wrap it," I instructed.

That took another fuckin' five minutes. I wanted a damn cigarette.

When he finally straightened out his leg, I wrapped his knee, through a lot of screaming on his part, and the fucker still couldn't stand up. I called Hayley in to help. Poor Annie had had enough of his crap for the day.

It took some co-ordination, but Hayley and I got him on his feet and handed him the crutches.

"You know you're gonna have to go down the steps on your ass like a baby, right? Ain't no way you're gonna make it on those crutches," I said.

It took a LOOONG time to get him downstairs. One slow step at time, with me holding his bad leg up by the bottom of his pants.

I finally got him maneuvered in front of the recliner and gave him a little shove. With a loud scream, he was down.

"Can I have a cigarette?" he asked. "Can I have some water and some aspirin?" he moaned. "You forgot the aspirin," he said after I handed him a glass of water. "What are we gonna have for dinner?" he asked. "Can you make me some hot dogs?" "Can I have some ketchup?" "Can I have the pee bottle?" On and on and on.

"Just leave me the fuck alone!" I wanted to scream.

When it was time to go to bed, he said he couldn't sleep in the recliner; it was making his back hurt. Fuck me! I would have to move his ass again.

I helped him get up and make his way to the couch. Twinkie was on the couch. She slept on the couch. She didn't want to move. While I found this hysterical, I wanted to go to bed. I coaxed the hundred-pound dog off the couch and helped him lay down.

On my way up the stairs, I heard his cries of agony. Twinkie had gone to the other end of couch and jumped up on his legs.

THE PINK FUZZY SOCK

He "broke his leg" on Friday morning. It was now Saturday night.

While I was out earlier that day, Hayley said she saw him walk to the bathroom and also walk to the back room to make a cigarette. She said he was only using one crutch. Was he making the whole thing up so he didn't have to find a job? I didn't know; he was a very good liar.

As soon as I got home (from a teenager's funeral, mind you, so I was in no fuckin' mood to deal with him), he started with the moaning and crying again. I didn't know what the hell to think. All I knew was that I was emotionally exhausted, and didn't want to go sit in a hospital for hours.

Around midnight, he was in agony, or so he said. I had given him the last of the ibuprofen. Hayley and I stood up and headed for the stairs to go to bed.

"I can't take it anymore. I need to go to the hospital," he cried.

"Danny, I don't even know if I can get you to the fuckin' car," I said sarcastically.

Soon, a screaming match broke out. Finally, I could take no more. I was taking him to the hospital just to prove his fuckin' leg wasn't broken...In the middle of the frigid, snow covered night...When all I wanted to do was sleep.

I got him his shoes. He needed my help getting them on; course he did. I got down there to put his shoes on and I noticed he was wearing one of his socks, and on the other foot, was one of Annie's pink, fuzzy socks. "Oh, well," I thought, and put his shoes on.

It took me and Hayley a while to get his big ass off the couch. He put his arm around Hayley for support, then lost his balance, and her face slammed into his moist armpit. The man had not showered in days; he was too busy throwin' up in my cups!

My poor little girl; she struggled to get her face loose, then looked at me with eyes bulging out of her head, her hand desperately fanning the stench away from her nose.

When we made it onto the front porch, I told Hayley to go back inside; it was freezing and I had this. But, apparently, I did not.

He made his way over to the two steps that would get him off the porch. We both looked down at them.

"I don't think you're gonna get down those steps on crutches," I said, shaking my head.

But he wanted to try anyway. I got in front of him and held out my arms, bracing myself to catch him if he fell.

Next thing I knew, he was falling. But backwards. The fuckin' crutches were flying up in the air; his eyes and toothless mouth were all as big as saucers. BOOM! Down he went. Sweet Baby Jesus, his screams were so loud, I don't know why the neighbors didn't come a runnin'.

I started coughing like a maniac, trying to cover my hysterical laughter. I knew it wasn't supposed to be funny; but it was.

The blinds on the window of the front door flew up; Hayley had come to find out what all the ruckus was about.

She looked down at him, her mouth fell open and she looked at me. I mimed what had happened. He was rolling around down on the floor, still screaming in pain. I saw her burst out laughing. Then he started to roll to face the door.

I started violently shaking my head "No!" at her. She saw he was gonna see her laughing and suddenly dropped to the floor; out of sight!

Seeing her there one second and gone the next made me laugh even harder and I just couldn't contain it.

He was screaming so loud; I don't know if he realized I was laughing or not.

I finally got him to skootch across the porch on his ass and get in a sitting position at the edge of the steps. Hayley had come out to help. The two of us managed to get him back on his crutches, on solid ground.

It was a very short walk to the street, but to him, it was a mile.

"Get me the office chair and we'll roll me to the car," he said.

So, Hayley went in to get it.

It was a lot harder to get him in that fuckin' chair than I thought it would be. When he was finally on it, we started to roll him down the walkway. We rolled him about a foot and a half, then the chair got stuck in the snow. It was twenty degrees outside, and there we were, stuck and freezing to death. The damn man weighed 180 pounds; there was no way in hell a kid and I could carry his ass.

Hayley said she had an idea. She walked around him, and with all her might, shoved the chair. It broke loose of the snow and screams ensued; his bad leg was dragging across the ground. But he was rolling!

We got him to the end of the walkway where my car was waiting in the middle of the street. Instead of shoveling from the porch to the driveway, he shoveled from the porch straight out to the street. I guess he didn't take his poopy medicine that day and the liver ammonia was fogging his brain.

We live on a very busy road, but it was around two in the morning, so I was hoping no drunk drivers would come and plow us down.

It was a noisy and difficult task to get him into the car because his leg wouldn't bend. There was so much crap on the back seat floor, we couldn't move his seat to give him more room. I went to the driver's side to try to pull him in, while Hayley stood on his side and pushed. No good. He couldn't get that bad leg into the car.

I was shivering my ass off and Hayley lips were turning blue. Finally, I said, "Fuck it." I reached over, grabbed his leg and yanked it on in. Oh, you would've thought I chopped his balls off or something. But, he was in! We were off to the ER; it was 2:30 in the fuckin' freezing morning.

He didn't speak to me on the car ride to the ER. This gave me time to reflect. Was I being evil? Yes, I was. But, I couldn't help it. Every day seemed to bring a new problem for this guy that somehow ended up to be my problem to solve. We were going on three months since I let him come home, and things were getting worse instead of better.

We had no money for the February bills since he refused to get a temporary job, so I had to pull more out of my ass and my IRA. I was ready to snap. Don't think it hadn't entered my mind to just say fuck everything and pack the girls up and run away from home, because it did.

I pulled up to the sliding ER doors and went in to get a wheelchair and some help. The lady at the front desk took one look at my haggard face and said, "What's wrong, honey?"

I told her I needed help getting my husband out of the car, that he had hurt his knee and he was helpless. She was shaking her head, saying men were such babies. I told her she didn't know the half of it.

Even with the male tech helping me, it still took us at least ten minutes to get goddamn broken Danny out and onto the wheelchair, him screaming the whole damn time.

His hair was greasy, he stunk, and he was wearing one pink, fuzzy sock. My nerves were shot, I was mad as hell and I was embarrassed to be seen with him. Oh, and he had left his teeth at home so he looked more like my grandfather than my husband.

After I parked the car, I went in to find him. Hopefully, they would do an x-ray, tell him his knee was sprained and send us the fuck home. But nothing in this life with Danny is easy.

I found him in his cubicle with a tech, a doctor and a nurse. They were cutting off the knee wrap. And good God, he had taken his shoes off and you could see his pink foot; what those people must have thought!

When they were done, I took a peak. His knee was swelled up like a party balloon. My eyes got big and I thought, "Oh, shit!"

"It wasn't swollen at all when I wrapped it," I said. And it really wasn't. If it had been, I would have taken him to a doctor earlier; but it had looked just the same as his other knee. I swear.

Well, they all gave me a look of disapproval; I guess because I didn't seem to have any sympathy for his pain and they thought I was a bitch.

While the doctor was examining his knee, and he was screaming, the nurse was trying to ask me questions. She didn't look sympathetic to my plight, so I was gonna make her understand.

"He did this to himself," I began. "I'm really not mean; I just can't take anymore."

Then I proceeded to list off his ailments for her: "cirrhosis of the liver, ulcer, arrhythmia, low platelet count, gall stones, hepatitis C, blown veins, crippling leg cramps and now this shit. I spent a month taking him to doctors. It's always something giving him an excuse not to go to work!"

My speech seemed to bring her over to my side. I guess his conditions gave her insight as to what the hell I had to deal with every fuckin' day of my life.

After x-rays, blood tests, the draining of his knee, and what seemed like ten hours, the doctor came back in. Danny had torn a ligament in his knee, and now it was infected. Mmm. I guess he was hurt after all; who knew?

They were gonna admit him so he could see the orthopedic surgeon in the morning. Great. Just fuckin' dandy. More time out of work for surgery recovery. And I just knew he was gonna turn this shit around and make it all my fault.

I stood up and announced I was going home; that it was way past my bedtime. I bent over and kissed his head and told him I would call when I woke up. I had no idea when that would be, because it was now 4:45 am and I still had to drive home.

As I was walking away, he tried to grab my hand, but it slipped out. I turned to look back and he was laying there, hand still stretched out, looking pitiful. I was half fuckin' delirious by that time, so I just waved bye, bye and kept on going. I guess I am a bitch.

TEETH VERSES TEETH

The next day, I called him. They had moved him to another hospital and he was waiting to have surgery.

Then he told me the doctor said it probably got infected because he waited too long to come in. Whoops.

I told him to call me back after surgery and he said he didn't have my number. I know. I've had this number for at least three years. He always remembered it when it was time to call me to pick him up from the fuckin' bus stop.

Then he told me he needed me to bring him his glasses and his teeth.

"Oh," I said. "Hayley said when she was cleaning her room, she only saw your bottom dentures on the dresser."

"Oh, no!" he whined, "Hayley cleaned her room? She probably threw them away."

"She didn't throw your fuckin' teeth away. Anyway, the trash bag's still up there. I'll find 'em."

"She probably stepped on them and broke them," he went on. And on and on.

I assured him I would find them; they probably just fell between the bed and the dresser.

Later, when Hayley got home from school, I told her we were gonna have to take daddy his glasses and his teeth. She told me again, there was only one denture up there. I said I would find the other one.

A little while later, Hayley told me she wanted to tell me the truth about something. She said while she was cleaning her room, she stepped on a tooth. Then she looked around, and on her bed was daddy's dentures, all broken up.

She hid them in her drawer because she didn't want the puppy to get in trouble. Fuckin' puppy-it chewed on everything!

"Oh, shit," I said. "Can we glue them back together?"

"Yes, if you want to do a puzzle," she said.

"Bring 'em down and let me see."

She handed me a pile of teeth and gums. There was no fuckin' way they were going back together.

I started examining them for bite marks and didn't see any. I made Hayley swear that she didn't step on them by accident.

Hayley and I were looking at them, trying to decide what the hell to do, when she said, "Aren't those bite marks?" I looked closer. Yes, indeed they were. I wrapped the broken pieces in a bag and threw them in the trash.

I decided to tell Danny HE must have knocked them onto the bed when he broke his leg, then fell on top of them and crushed them; he was in so much pain, he must not have noticed.

THE PATIENT FROM HELL

They went into his knee with a camera to find out what was going on. By this time, his whole leg was swollen and he said his nuts were so big, he couldn't spread his legs any further. I found this hard to believe; his nuts weren't that big to begin with.

Turns out, it wasn't a torn ligament after all, just some torn cartilage. They washed his knee out to remove the floating cartilage, and to try to get rid of the infection. They also discovered he had arthritis in his knee; one more ailment to add to the list; he was a fuckin' mess.

I asked the nurse if I had caused this infection by waiting to bring him in. She said, most likely I did not; it would have gotten infected anyway. Whew, she let me off the hook.

Then she said, "it just might not have been as bad." Well, damn.

I called Danny that night to check on him and see how he was feeling. As soon as he answered, he started bitchin' about his nurse. She was a Russian, she was a bitch and she wouldn't give him any food.

Then she was there with him, and I could hear their conversation. She did sound like a bitch, but it was probably because she had been dealing with his ass all day.

I listened to them go at it for a while about food, ice and his pain; then she left.

"You see what I mean?" Danny asked, looking for my sympathy. I was just glad she was dealing with him instead of me; at least she was getting paid.

"Honey, you need to be nice to your nurse; she said she was doing her best."

"They aren't doing anything for me. I tell them I need something and they disappear for two hours," he ranted. "She better bring me some food; I haven't eaten in eighteen hours."

"Oh, that's right; they won't let you eat before surgery," I remembered.

"Yeah, no shit," he smart-mouthed me. "Will you please bring me my teeth tomorrow?"

Damn, there he went with the teeth again.

"I'll try. I have to work all day."

"Forget it," he said, "Just mail 'em to me," and he hung up the phone.

Coco **NUTS**

The next day, he told me they were gonna to have to go back in and clean his knee again.

"When?" I asked.

"In a day or two, they want the swelling to go down."

I had been avoiding going to the hospital to see Danny because I didn't want to tell him the dog ate his fuckin' teeth. I talked to him on the phone every day, but changed the subject when he said he really needed those teeth.

On day five of his hospital stay, he had the nurse call and ask me to come visit him, so I guessed I was gonna have to bite the bullet and drive up there. He was supposed to have surgery to clean out his knee again after 2:00, so I told her I'd come in around 4:30. He still had a very bad infection.

When Hayley got home from school, I told her we were gonna go visit daddy. She looked at me with fear in her eyes; she didn't want him to kill her dog. I told her we would take his bottom teeth and his glasses, and just tell him we hadn't found the top ones yet. I put them in a bubble envelope and sealed it.

When we got to the hospital, his surgery had been pushed back to 6:30 pm. We found him in a pre-op room, bitchin' at the poor nurse; not the Russian, another one.

"Look what they've done to me," he said, lifting both arms that were covered with bruises.

"Danny, your veins are shot; it's not their fault."

"No, I guess it's my fault. I'm just a piece of shit. Everything's my fault, like you said," his words attacked me.

"I didn't say that; calm down," I said, looking to see if the nurse had heard.

"They won't give me any pain medicine," he complained.

I looked at the IV drip and said, "your medicine's right there in the IV."

"Oh. Well, it isn't working. I'm in pain and my nuts are still swollen."

"Well, I don't know what your nuts have to do with your knee."

He went on complaining, mean as bear. Hayley whispered in my ear that now might be a good time to tell him about the teeth, but I said no. He was going into surgery and I didn't want to give him any more stress; see? I'm nice.

I was trying to be understanding, but it was hard. Hayley got tired of listening to him bitch, so she said she was going to the bathroom.

As soon as she left the room, Danny whipped off his blanket, and said, "Look at my nuts!"

178

Sweet Jesus! The two had become one and it was the size of a fuckin' coconut!

"Can't they put some ice on that bitch?" I exclaimed, shocked by the size and biting my tongue again so the laughter wouldn't escape.

"Feel how heavy they are," he demanded, cupping the giant sac.

I didn't want to; but I did. It was heavy, all right. And it felt like a warm water balloon. Looked like one too; all giggly, skin pulled tight, and what was left of his poor penis was just laying there like the part of the balloon you tie off.

THEY'RE KEEPIN' HIM!!!

When I left Danny in pre-op, I found his room and left the envelope with his glasses and bottom teeth.

He called me the next day to tell me that they cleaned inside his knee again, and if it didn't get better this time, they would have to do real surgery on it.

Then he complained about his teeth.

First he asked where the top ones were; I said I hadn't found them yet. Then he informed me the bottom ones were broken. They didn't look broke to me, but what do I know about fake teeth? I know I need a few for my own damn mouth, but since the dog ate his, and he had zero, he took priority.

A couple more days went by; I didn't visit. I didn't want to sit there and listen to him bitch about everything including his giant balls. The knee cleanings didn't work, so he had real surgery. And while enjoying his hospital stay, he contracted a staph infection and would need intravenous antibiotics for eight weeks.

They put a pic-line in his vein and because he had a history of drug use, wouldn't let him give himself the medicine at home. No one would take the liability of homeboy running around town with an open vein.

But that meant weeks of more peace for me and the girls. This time while he was gone we painted the kitchen Bubble Gum Pink.

EXTENDED VACAY!

The antibiotic Danny was on was hurting his kidneys; another ailment for the growing list. They had to start over with another drug. He couldn't put any pressure on his knee and his nuts were still huge. I didn't know if he'd ever come home.

He was mad because I wasn't coming to see him every day, but I didn't have gas money for that shit. He said he was bored and lonely. You'd think he'd be on cloud nine; sleeping all the time, lying in bed watching TV, having someone wait on him hand and foot, and not having to go to work. It should've been paradise for him. It was heaven for us!

LIVIN' IN THE 1800'S

While Danny was living it up in the hospital, my wash machine broke. Probably karma biting me in the ass for not visiting him enough. I was used to appliances breaking, but usually drunk Danny was here to try to save the day-like with the clothes dryer and the spider web of clothes hanging in my back yard.

We aren't like normal people who can go to the department store and buy a new appliance when one breaks; nor can we afford to call a repairman in. We have Danny.

When I bought my house, the seller just flipped it, so I had all new, high grade appliances; but no appliance is made to last forever.

One by one, the appliances broke. We never had any fucking money so we made due with what we could do without, or Danny rigged them half-ass to get us by till we could find a free replacement.

When the dishwasher stopped draining, he tried to fix it, but to no avail. I found a free one on freecycle.org one day. After we went to the trouble of borrowing a truck, picking it up and installing it, that one wouldn't drain either! The new neighbors renovated their kitchen with all new stainless appliances. Danny swore the old neighbor had replaced all the appliances to sell the house, so when those went out to the curb, we trash-picked the dishwasher.

Guess what? Bitch wouldn't drain. I've had dishpan hands for at least four years now.

While I was waiting for the dishwasher to be fixed, the stovetop grill on the Jenn Air went out, so I was left with two burners. That was fine until the glass on the front of the oven door fell off. Don't ask me how that happened; I don't know. Drunk Danny was probably cooking a snack and broke the damn thing. So he put it back on with duct tape. It looked like shit.

One day, I was cooking and the duct tape let go. The huge piece of thick glass fell on my damn toes and almost broke them. The door still had a metal front, so we didn't put the glass back on.

Well, without the glass, the handle eventually fell off, so we had to grab the side of the door to open it with an oven mitt. Then, somehow the spring latch that held the door open so you could put your fuckin' cake inside, broke. Annie was always forgetting this little tidbit. Whenever she needed to bake something, she was forever letting go of the door and the bitch would slam to the floor.

Sometimes, I'd forget the door was just metal now, get too close, and burn my cooch.

Then the fuckin' fridge started acting up. Either the refrigerator side was too cold and would freeze everything, or the freezer was too warm and everything would melt. We could NOT afford a new refrigerator, so we trucked over to the Re-Store to look for a used one.

There was one fridge in our price range, but I didn't think it would fit in the space between the cabinets where the old one was. I had told Danny to take measurements before we left, but he was drinking, so he forgot.

We bought it anyway; he swore it would fit. It took Danny and two neighbors to get that thing in my kitchen, and what do know? Bitch didn't fit. We couldn't take it back, so now we had this monster size fridge. We stuck it in the back room adjacent to the kitchen and it took up a quarter of the room. And there was no plumbing in that room for the ice maker.

Now, Danny likes his beer on ice cubes and he wasn't accustomed to using ice trays, so he decided since the fuckin' dishwasher didn't work anyway, he'd just run that water line to the new fridge in the back room.

Not caring what the hell things looked like, and not caring that I was trying to make our half-ass kitchen look cute, he didn't try to hide the yellowed water tube; he just ran it right across the fuckin' floor for everyone to see.

It stayed like that until one of the animals chewed a hole in it and he didn't have his precious ice. He replaced the tube, still ran it across the floor, but later, the icemaker broke anyway.

Later, the front coil burner on the stove went out. So now, I had no dishwasher, had to go to another room to get something out of the refrigerator, and had to cook on a stove with one burner.

185

Since I'm short, and the working burner was in the back, I had to lean over to stir with my butt sticking out so I wouldn't burn my coochie on the fucked-up broken oven door.

The Re-Store said they never got Jenn Air's, and a brand new one cost thousands of dollars. Since our stove was in an island in the middle of the room, it had a down draft; we couldn't just buy any old stove.

I went to Home Depot and bought a new coil, but, it didn't work when I plugged it in. I didn't realize with a Jenn Air, you had to replace the whole two burner unit.

So, Danny and I went to the appliance store. Before we left, I looked for the serial number, but for the life of me, couldn't find it; it was probably on the broken part of the door we had thrown away. We decided that that model would be at the store and we could just tell the salesman.

But my damn stove was ten years old and they didn't have one like it in the showroom. We searched the catalog with the salesman and found one that looked kind of like it, but not exactly. The part was almost $200, so I said we would come back. I would search the basement for the manual; I was sure I had it. Just then, my cellphone rang, so I went outside to talk.

I thought fuckin' Danny was behind me, but, hell no. By the end of my phone conversation, he came strolling out of the store with a big ole bag. He said he bought the part for the stove that was close to ours, and we'd return it if it didn't work. Fine, I thought, and we went home.

I was tending to the kids while he was installing the part.

He came out of the kitchen and told me it didn't work.

"Okay, we'll just take it back," I told him.

"We can't," he said.

The drunk idiot had broken the part! Our stove had 2 holes, but the part had three prongs. So, instead of putting the damn thing back in the box, he sawed off the extra prong and wondered why in the hell it didn't work. $200 fuckin' dollars down the drain! I could have killed him!

A few months later, I found a plain old electric stove at a yard sale for thirty bucks. It didn't have a down draft, but by this time I was desperate; I was tired of eating microwave food. I brought it home for Danny to install.

When he removed the Jenn Air, there was a big fan attached to the floor for the down draft. He got me and made me look. I said I didn't give a shit; take it out, I need a stove.

So he kicked at it until it came loose. The back of the yard sale stove leans up against a breakfast bar, and is about an inch and a half higher than the bar. It looks like shit, but at least the stove is in good working order.

Now, my fuckin' wash machine is broken and Danny's in the hospital with his giant balls! The machine goes through all the cycles, but won't drain. Annie and I watched a YouTube video and tried to fix the damn thing ourselves, but we couldn't.

So, when I don't have time to drag laundry to my mom's or sister's house, we pretend we live in the 1800's and do it by hand. I wash the clothes in the sink, then haul them to the dryer, water dripping on the floor the whole way. I've rubbed two huge blisters on my hand from ringing the damn clothes out!

I tried to wash the towels in the bathtub, but when I lifted the first one to ring it, it was so heavy I threw my back out.

LESSONS LEARNED-NOT!

It was almost time for Danny to come home. He would emerge from the hospital clean and sober, probably for the first time in his adult life (or so I thought-I'll get to that later). He would have medical problems for the rest of his life, but hopefully, where drugs and alcohol were concerned, he'd learned his lesson.

Danny never learned his lesson before; but I could dream. Even simple lessons, like never leave your food unattended when you live in a zoo. The first time he left his dinner on the coffee table to go to the bathroom, we were dog sitting for a friend.

He came back into the living room just in time to see his plate empty and our house guest licking his chops. Danny was furious; he had worked hard on that sandwich. And he had used the end of the loaf of bread to make it; no more till momma drove her ass to the store.

Twinkie, our lab, was good; she never stole his food. Either she was afraid of him, or too lazy to leave her chair. Years passed before the puppy came along; the very bad little dog, Teeny.

Danny must have forgotten about the other dog that stole his dinner, because he left a plate unattended again. He went to the bathroom. If he hadn't drank so damn much, he might not have had to pee all the time.

Anyway, Danny came back into the living room as the puppy ran past him with his hot dog hanging out of its mouth, bun and all. Teeny got his food a few more times before the dumbass started putting his plate on the counter.

But then he forgot we had cats. By this time, we had a few cats.

One night, drunk Danny put his dinner on the counter so Teeny wouldn't get it. He came back from the bathroom and found three cats fancy feasting on his plate of spaghetti. He started yelling. I started laughing.

Our cats are rude. And very brave. Sometimes when he's eating at the coffee table, one of them will hop up and try to sneak food from right under his nose. If he wasn't too drunk, he would notice, grab the cat and sling it across the room. Then it just came back.

One time, he was cooking fish in a frying pan. He was seasoning it and doing his best to make it restaurant quality. But, he had to go to the bathroom. He came back to find two cats chowing away at the fish, right out of the hot pan.

He also never learned that he couldn't drink liquor with a belly full of beer or he was gonna fall down. Every time he mixed the two: Timber! Fucker would fall right over like a chopped tree and bust his head.

Another lesson he refused to learn: never weld a car without wearing goggles. A few times a year, he'd have to go to the ER and get metal taken out of his eye. One time he almost went blind. The doctor was trying to remove a sliver of metal with his tweezers, when Danny felt a gush of water run down his face and heard the doctor say "Oh, shit."

Danny's fuckin' eye had popped. I wasn't aware an eye could pop, but it can. Danny looked like a goddamn pirate for a while, and of course, couldn't work because his peripheral vision was fucked. More money lost because he didn't do what he was supposed to.

He never learned that even if it's slow at work, and ya ain't got nothin' to do, you can't just leave for the day or you'll lose your job. I lost count of how many jobs he lost for just up and leaving in the middle of the day. Guess that beer was calling him.

He also never learned how attached Hayley got to her pets and when one died, he should just hide it in a trashcan and pretend it ran away. Boo was Hayley's cat. She loved that stupid cat with all her heart and Danny knew it.

One drunk night, we were all watching TV, when Danny jumped up and ran out the front door. What he saw, that none of us did, was a car driving by, swerve and almost hit our tree.

He came back through the door with Boo in his arms. Petting it he said, "Kitty's gonna sleep now."

We looked at him like he was crazy. Then Hayley asked for her cat.

Continuing to pet it, he said, "No; kitty gonna sleep now."

I hadn't been paying much attention and told him to give her the damn cat. Then I looked up at him and noticed the cat wasn't moving. Alarmed, I asked if it was dead.

Still petting the corpse, he said, "yes, a car hit it. She's gonna sleep now."

Hayley lost her fucking mind. I started screaming at him for bringing it in the house in front of her.

"What the hell were you thinking?"

"Why ya yellin' at me, I didn't hit it?"

HELL CAME HOME

Homecoming day arrived. Yay. The night before, Hayley told Annie that our vacation was over. It surely was.

During checkout, two and half months after I took him to the ER for his knee, his nurse gave me all the medications that were left in his drawer with instructions; it was even more confusing than the last batch of thirteen prescriptions he got sent home with. She also gave me a list of physical therapists in our area; he would need months of physical therapy for his bum knee.

What I didn't know at the time, and would soon find out, was that Danny might not be addicted to alcohol anymore, but he was now addicted to OxyContin. He, of course, blamed that shit on the hospital.

On the morning of the fourth day after he came home, he informed me that he only had one dose of pain killers left and I needed to call the doctor to get some more. I dialed the number and handed him the damn phone; I wasn't his mother (although you wouldn't know that since I had to dial the damn phone).

They informed him that they couldn't give him anymore; that he would have to go to a long term pain management doctor and gave us the phone number. Well, the pain management place didn't take our poor people insurance and wanted $750 for just the first visit. I told the druggie he was shit out of luck. He didn't like that response.

He got back on the phone with the knee doctor and bitched and cried about his pain until they agreed to give him a two-week supply; but that was it!

I hauled his ass back to the doctor to pick up the prescription. Since his pain killers were narcotics, they couldn't just call it in.

We got to the pharmacy and I asked if he wanted to go in, but of course, it would hurt his knee too much to hike across the parking lot.

I went in and handed the lady the prescription. She said to hold on while she checked to see if she had it.

She came back and told me she couldn't refill the oxys for three more days. I asked if I could get them from another pharmacy or if they were in a master computer. She said that narcotics were in a master and I wouldn't be able to refill them anywhere. Apparently, Danny had taken a seven-day supply in four days; idiot!

Now, every time Danny got fired, it was always the same; he would call me and say: "Bad news. They let me go. Come and get me."

I got back in the car and lit a cigarette.

"Bad news," I said. "They won't give you the OxyContin for three more days. You can go in and ask if you don't believe me."

Major groan from the passenger seat. I took a drag off my cigarette and sat there in great satisfaction. God it felt good to finally be the one to deliver the "bad news."

"Let's go to Giant and fill it there," he said, brightening up.

"Can't. Controlled substances are in a master computer. You can't get anywhere."

I thought he was gonna cry.

Outdoor Air Conditioning

When we got home, I told him I needed him to walk the perimeter of our yard and tell me which pieces of junk were actually tools and which pieces I could throw away.

When we got to the far side of the house, we found some of the gutters we had purchased for the refinance that never happened a few years before because the dumbass had gotten fired before the loan was approved.

I said, "there's the gutters you never put up."

"I put some of them up; those were for the roof and I didn't have a ladder high enough. I put up the ones I could reach."

I looked up to check and what do you supposed I saw laying on the lower, slanted roof of the back room? A fuckin' huge air conditioner unit; just sitting there, rusting.

"What the hell is that doing up there," I asked.

"When it broke, I pushed it out the bedroom window. I thought it would slide to the ground, but it got stuck on gutter," he explained.

I thought he had gotten rid of that thing two years ago; I had no idea it had been sitting up there. We had just excelled from redneck to white trash.

There was no way I could get that thing down; it was very heavy. There was no way helpless, feeble Danny was gonna be able to climb up there and get it down. If I forced him to try, he was sure to fall off the ladder on purpose and really break his leg (or his neck. Hmm? Just kidding).

The next door neighbors would have to look at it a while longer; I'm sure we were a fun topic at their cookouts.

"I'VE NEVER SEEN SUCH A THING!"

I had told Danny that he needed to use his two-week supply of Oxys to wean himself off; that he wasn't getting any more. But drug addicts are very resourceful and he was hooked on the damn things. He got on the phone and started calling all his old druggie friends until he found one that had a pain management doctor that was cheap enough for us to afford without insurance.

He made an appointment for the next day, not giving a shit that I had to work. He informed me that he had to have the pills if I ever wanted him to work again. So I rearranged my schedule.

It took almost two fuckin' hours and God knows how much gas to get to the doctor. When we got there, we waited for a while, then they took him back to take a drug test. Then we waited some more for the results.

When the doctor took him back to examine him, I went too. I sat in the chair while the doc took his vitals and talked to him about his pain. I was bored until the doctor laid him down, then called me over five seconds later.

"Come here, I want to show you something," the doctor said to me.

I walked over to the exam table and he said "watch".

The doc took his little flashlight, stuck it up one of Danny's nostrils and the light came beamin' out the other one. I was confused so I looked up his nose. There was a pencil eraser size hole up his nose where cartilage was supposed to be separating his nostrils.

"How the hell did that get there?" I asked.

Turns out, the idiot had snorted so much cocaine in his youth it had eaten through the inside of his nose. There would be no Oxys for Danny. The doctor wasn't willing to break the law for Danny's pain. Thank God! I could save some damn money.

JELL-O AND THROW-UP

The weaning of the Oxys didn't go too well. Instead of making them last, Danny ran out of them before he was supposed to. No surprise there. Then he started to withdraw. It was pretty fuckin' gross for me and the kids and pretty painful for him-or so he said. After a couple days, he started whining to go to the ER-the last fuckin' thing I wanted to spend my time doin'.

He said he needed some narcotics to stop the symptoms. I knew I had some pain killers the dentist had given me years before that I never took and stashed away. I went to my secret hiding place and what do you know? They were gone. When I took away his beer at one time or another, the bloodhound must have found them. I was pissed.

I did find some very old pain killers I had for Twinkie when she hurt her leg. I googled them and it didn't say people couldn't take them. I gave him two and a glass of water.

A few hours after administering dog pills to Danny, I went in the kitchen to make myself some Jell-O. I piled the whip cream on high and grabbed a spoon.

Taking my first delicious bite as I walked into the living room, I was horrified to see puke spraying out of Danny's mouth and him struggling to get out of my chair on his bad knee. It was like the fuckin' exorcist in there.

I did an about face and ran back to the kitchen before I started to choke.

Poor Hayley was in the bathroom, trying to poop, when he started banging on the door for her to get out.

She came running into the kitchen with her face all screwed up in disgust while I was dumping my Jell-O down the garbage disposal.

I threw a roll of paper towels on his seat, hoping he would get the hint, then Hayley and I ran up the stairs to escape the wretched noises pouring out of the bathroom.

THE NOT SO HELPFUL COP

The next morning, I got the kids off to school. I was headed to the kitchen for my second cup of coffee and I heard, "Did you call the doctor?" I didn't know he was there and it scared the shit out of me.

I had decided that he needed to go to the family doctor to get something, anything, to lessen his withdraw symptoms. I had better things to do than spend time going to more doctors, but he was throwing up on everything.

On the way down the highway to his appointment, I heard a gagging noise next to me. I asked if he was gonna throw up and he told me to pull over. I said there was nowhere to pull and handed him a wad of napkins. He threw up in his mouth and I don't know if he swallowed it or spit in the napkin; I wasn't looking.

He told me to pull over again, so I pulled into the exit lane and hit my hazards. He proceeded to throw up out the door three or four times. I was having bad flashbacks of the drunk, hangover days, when I looked in my rear view and there was a cop getting out of his car.

"Great, now the cops are here," I said in an angry tone.

"Are you guys okay," the cop asked me.

"He's getting sick," I said. I didn't know if I was gonna get in trouble for pulling over in the exit lane or not.

"Does he need an ambulance?" the officer asked.

"No," Danny spoke up. He proceeded to tell the cop he was withdrawing from pain killers; that he had just had knee surgery.

"Are they really strong ones, like Oxys?" the officer asked.

"Yeah, Oxys," Danny said.

Then the very nice, concerned officer informed Danny that he could take some very addicting METHADONE to make him feel better and Danny's watery eyes lit up. I swear to God, I wanted to pull his gun out of his holster and shoot his ass.

I'm Done. Finally.

The gleam in his eyes at the mention of methadone made me finally realize he was always gonna be addicted to something and it would eventually destroy my life as well as his. I made the decision to get a divorce. But I had to wait until he at least had a job or I would be the fuckin' bitch that put a sick man out on the street.

After five more weeks of him withdrawing from OxyContin, sleeping eighteen hours a day and watching old movies, he finally found a job-one I would have to drive him to.

When the first paycheck came in and I finally had some damn money, I thought about letting him stay until he either got fired again or I caught him self-medicating with something he wasn't supposed to have. That was until the mail came one day.

In all the useless efforts to get the man his driver's license back, I had added him to my car insurance. My stupid agent told me this would be alright. Well, it wasn't.

When I opened what I thought to be my premium bill, it was actually a letter from my insurance company. It informed me that even though I had been paying them for car insurance for the past thirty-eight years, regretfully they were dropping me because my husband's license had been revoked/suspended. I lost my fucking mind!

My friend came over while I was in the throes of securing new, costlier car insurance which I in turn had to bundle with new home owner's insurance to bring the price down. When I got off the phone and told her what happened, she asked me if I was gonna wait until I lost everything before I got rid of him or did I want to do it now? I said now.

Knowing he had nowhere to go and no friends to call, he would probably end up sleeping in a bush again. I found one of Hayley's old backpacks and we started to pack him up for a few days of camping. It was summertime so he wouldn't freeze to death, but it was raining that day. We found a nice plastic tablecloth so he could make a tent and a big black trash bag that he could wear as a raincoat after we cut head and arm holes in it.

I rolled him a pack of homemade cigarettes and dumped a bunch of ibuprofen in a baggie. We packed enough clothes for three days and added a throw blanket for him to lay on. I didn't want him to starve so we went through the cabinets and stuffed some appropriate food in the bag. I remembered to put his teeth glue in there too.

Before I zipped the backpack, I wrote him a note saying we were over, put in his credit card that had $150 left on it and added $60 in cash.

My friend drove so I could make this quick. I asked her what I was supposed to say and she said not to say anything, just hand him the bag.

I walked into his garage and found him power sanding a car, his back to me.

"Danny!" I yelled over the sound of the machine.

He turned around and saw me holding out the backpack with a sad look on my face.

"What? You're throwing me out again?" he asked. I just nodded my head and put the backpack on the ground.

Then I ran.

I jumped in my friend's still running car and yelled, "Go, go, go!"

We had to dodge a bunch of parked cars to get out of there so we couldn't go fast.

I looked back and saw him hobblin' on his bad leg as fast as he could after us and heard him screaming at the top of his lungs that we were both man-hating cunts.

Escaping the parking lot, my whole world brightened.

A POEM

Danny got run over by a lawnmower

Cutting grass one day when he was lit

You may think I should feel pity for him

But I just thought, Oh Hell No-Fuck that shit!

The End